SWIMMING WITH SPIES

CHRYSTYNA LUCYK-BERGER

SWIMMING WITH SPIES

SCHOLASTIC PRESS / NEW YORK

ISBN 978-93-5954-519-6
This reprint edition, December 2024
Book design by Omou Barry
Printed at Shree Maitrey Printech Pvt. Ltd., Noida

To Sharon Davis of Cleveland Elementary, North Minneapolis

It all started with your hand, your guidance, your encouragement;

you were simply what a teacher is supposed to be.

CHAPTER 1

The Heart and the Kidney

I'm almost too tired to do Ilya's homework when the alarm beneath my pillow goes off. It nearly took me the whole night to finish my own illustration for biology and it'll be even harder to do Ilya's.

Everyone knows that drawing badly isn't something I do well. But Ilya Ilyich can't draw, so this has to look convincing. The twenty hryvnia I'll get for doing his homework is another twenty hryvnia closer to getting my bus ticket to Moscow.

I told Cedric about my plan once.

"Sofiya, what would you even do if you found her?" he asked.

I didn't know the answer then. Now I do. I would ask Mama why she ran away from home.

Along the walls of my bedroom, I've hung up string to clip my sketches and drawings onto. I've started a second row of string on the wall across from me, and will stretch some more when I need it. It looks like chaos, but I know where every single drawing is. Even the ones I keep hidden.

Neptune pushes into my room. With wet, snow-crusted

paws, he jumps onto the bed, purring so loudly, I'm afraid he'll wake up Tato in the next room. But the cat curls up and quiets down. The way he's shaped against my thigh makes him look like a kidney. And that's how I get the idea for Ilya's assignment. I'm going to draw a gray kidney with two pointy ears and whiskers. And maybe I'll do a detail of Neptune's front paw. Our biology teacher gives extra credit for stuff like that. Extra credit for kids like Ilya is worth a lot, which means my price just went up.

I'm nearly done when I hear Tato turn on the shower. From Neptune's tail on the page, I quickly draw a curved line and cross it over another line labeling Neptune's rump—an absolute no-no in scientific labeling—and write in Ukrainian, хвіст, and in Russian, хвост, but really messy so that the teacher will believe it's Ilya's writing. Then I quickly slip the sketch pad into my book bag before Tato comes out of the shower.

If my father catches me doing someone else's homework, it'll mean big trouble. Even if I argue that half the boys from 6C pay real money to the kids from 6A to do their homework for them, he'll give me the "Principle of the Matter" lecture followed by the "We Don't Break the Rules" lecture. The principle really is that Ilya Ilyich Chaban and his gang from 6C come from rich families, so they can afford to pay. We kids from 6A are considered the smart kids. So, instead of letting those 6C kids mob us, we earn cash. I'm not breaking the rules. I'm bending them. It's science, pure classification. I'm just looking at it from a different perspective.

Babushka says that turning a question over and over is the foundation of science, and to dissect that question from all angles is how we find the answers. In biology, our sixth form is learning to illustrate plants, animals, bacteria, even amoebae from different perspectives. Our focus this week is on the bird's-eye view, which means we're looking at our subjects from above. Afterward, we have to make perfectly straight lines and correctly label all the parts of our subjects.

Carefully observing, then neatly categorizing and labeling everything, is how a scientist makes sense of what she sees around her. Which is why I am going to be one. *Dr. Sofiya Oleksandrivna Len, Veterinarian.* Like Babushka. Or *Dr. Sofiya Oleksandrivna Len, Marine Biologist*, which is what my tato was studying to be before he met my mother. By the time I was born, he was a dolphin trainer, and now he is the director of the Sevastopol dolphinarium. Whichever it is, I'm going to be a scientist because everything—nature, friends, school, my family, everything I see—is messy and Dr. Sofiya Oleksandrivna Len is going to make sense of it all.

Tato walks in wearing a bathrobe. His hair is wrapped up in a man bun. Even in the winter, he's tan.

"Good morning, Sofiya. Have you had breakfast already?"

"I'll take one of Babushka's *pyrizhky* with me. I have to go or I'll be late."

He produces my brush from behind his back, and I groan. I have gnarled blond curls and I hate brushing my hair. It hurts my head. But I drop my bag by the door and hurry into the steamy bathroom and untangle the ends, then put on my wool cap over the rest of the disaster.

In the kitchen, there is the scent of almonds and apples as the small blender whirs and chops. Tato is making a smoothie and Neptune is winding his way around his legs, meowing in that gravelly old tomcat voice. He's waiting for the *pop-squish-suck* sound that signals breakfast. When it comes, I hold my nose at the puke-stench of chicken hearts and livers.

I pull on my boots and throw on my coat, ready to run out the back door. But Tato comes over, stuffs the entire oval apricot *pyrizhok* into my mouth, and points to my bag.

"You need to finish those illustrations for biology today. You're still doing the dolphins, right?"

My heart kind of freezes. I make a sound around the pastry in my mouth that might be interpreted as "Uh-huh," because Tato forgot that my sketches are due today. That's what happens when he spends an entire night playing chess with Ivan Markovych. He loses track of time.

Besides, I know all the dolphins from front to back, and up and down. For this assignment, I drew Colin from memory. He's a *Tursiops truncatus ponticus*, a Black Sea bottlenose dolphin. If Tato looks into my sketchbook now and spots the awful kidney-shaped illustration of Neptune, he'll ask questions.

He chucks me under the chin. "Can't wait to see what you do. The illustration you drew of the heart was really good."

I redden, and bite down on the pastry, apricot jam filling my mouth. I make that noise again that Tato might think is "Uh-huh" or "Thanks." Then I escape.

As I wheel my bicycle to the gate, I catch sight of Neptune in the bay window, his gray shadow and yellow eyes peering out at me. He stands up, arches his back, and makes his tail into a question mark before sitting down again.

There is a fresh layer of snow on the sidewalk, and the street sign is caked with clumps of it. We live on *Вулиця Рибочка—Vul. Rybochka*—Little Fish St. At the end of the road, I take a left and bike along the waterfront, which in February is icy, cold, and empty. At the Monument to the Sunken Ships, the Ukrainian flag—sky blue above golden yellow—snaps in a stiff breeze. I spot the sleek gray-green ships skimming the waters on the horizon and coast to a stop to watch them.

With stiff fingers, I wrench out my observation journal and

a pencil from the front pocket of my schoolbag. Underneath yesterday's note, I write:

Tuesday, 18th of February, 2014. 1 freight ship. 1 scout boat. 2 fishing boats. 6 seagulls. Wind from the northwest. Cold to the bone.

I get back on my bike. Across the promenade, in an empty parking lot, Ivan Markovych's yellow-and-white food truck is still locked up tight. His three pit bulls—Musty, Monk, and Marble—are curled up beneath the caravan on old plaid sofa cushions and dirty blankets. They keep guard all night long. Marble, my favorite, raises his head and thumps his tail as I pedal by. Along the side of the caravan, Ivan Markovych has a sampling of the postcards he sells. They all depict Sevastopol in the summer.

Kids don't run away from home because they actually believe they're going somewhere better. Not for real, anyway. They do it to get attention. But adults run away all the time. Sometimes they run right here to Sevastopol. They bring their families down to the Crimean Peninsula in the summer, and swamp the beaches to escape the heat in the big cities. They buy postcards of dolphins and porpoises, eat Ivan Markovych's famous fish tacos (five stars on Trip Advisor according to a half-peeled sticker in the window), go swimming in the warm Black Sea, and talk about what a dream it would be to live here year-round.

Those same tourists are never here in the winter, though, when the wind and the waves throw up icy sprays of sea-foam. But I don't think my mother ran away to Russia because of the weather. After all, in the winter, Moscow is much colder than Sevastopol.

CHAPTER 2

Sharks and Dolphins

As I pull into the schoolyard, Cedric pushes away from the stone banister and raises his hand in a salute. He is shivering in a coat that is too tight for his round hips. The clock above says we have five minutes before the bell calls us inside.

Gathered at the top of the stairs is the Russian Hill clique from 6C. They are all wearing those winter coats that look like space suits with a patch or number on the breast. Babushka says that these are the kids from families who moved to Sevastopol when it was purely a military base. Ilya Ilyich Chaban belongs to this gang. I call them Ilya and the Idiots.

I keep watch on the clique as I lock up my bike, but they don't take note of me. Cedric and I are in the 6A class, the gifted students. In other words, and according to the laws of social science, we're the ones who always get picked on, which is part of the reason we're best friends. We've learned that if we stick together, "Ilya and the Idiots" get spread out too thinly. Cedric meets me halfway and we share our secret handshake—fist bump, high five, waggle the fingers and dance them back.

That's when Ilya notices us. He narrows his eyes at Cedric and leans over the banister.

"Is that a tribal dance where you come from, Cedric?"

I step in front of my friend, and Ilya jeers at me. He has sandy brown hair, and there's a swath of bang that hangs over one eye that he always flips back with the shake of his head.

"Your friend should go back to Africa," Ilya taunts.

Cedric tugs at my backpack, just once, like he doesn't want anybody else to see that he's trying to stop me.

"You're a racist, Ilya!" I shout. "Cedric was born here, just like you. Why don't *you* go back to Krasnodar, where your father is from? Just pack up and take the ferry back to Russia!"

My heart is beating in my throat. It always does when I talk back before thinking it through. Which is a lot of times. Babushka says I have my mother's temperament. Tato says that can be a good thing.

Maybe not this time, though. The boys from 6C are all making noise and big Os with their mouths, pushing Ilya to retaliate. There are six in total. He shakes off the group around him and folds his arms.

"Look at that," he sneers. "The Little Mermaid thinks she can tell us what to do."

The boys above laugh. "Little Mermaid" *is* funny, and I laugh, too. Ilya takes a step back and frowns. He looks around, like he suddenly needs a signal from his gang about what to do next. That makes me realize, *I got him!* He doesn't know what to do about my laughter.

But then Cedric pushes forward. His eyes are wide with rage. He puffs out his cheeks.

"If she's the Little Mermaid," he shouts, "you're the crab under the sea!"

Everyone is wound up now. Everyone is throwing words like sharp pebbles in both Russian and Ukrainian.

I step in front of Cedric, because this is not going to turn out well, and say in Ukrainian, "I'll handle this." Then to the clique, I shout in Russian, "Hey, Ilya Ilyich. I've got your homework done! You owe me twenty—"

But Ilya makes a guttural sound and leaps off the stairs. His friends are on his heels. I spread my feet apart.

Tato once said that if I want to command attention, I need to make myself bigger. Animals do that all the time. It's why dogs raise their hackles, why cats arch their backs and fluff out their tails, and blowfish, well, they blow themselves up.

I move my book bag between Ilya and me, and put my hand out. "Twenty hryvnia. That was our deal."

"How about I don't beat your bug-eyed friend here and we call it even?" Ilya says dangerously. He obviously doesn't want anyone to know about our arrangement.

My neck is really hot beneath my scarf. "How about you give me the twenty hryvnia or you fail your biology class?"

Cedric steps right next to me. "You better do what Sofiya says or you'll get in big trouble with—"

Ilya is a blur and when I turn around, he and Cedric are tumbling on the ground. And there we go. Any kid in any schoolyard knows what happens next. First, the shouts of surprise and a thrilled cheer from the other students. Then they build a tight circle around the fight, screaming and pounding their fists into their hands.

There are only two sides to choose from. Either they are cheering for the big dog or they know what it's like to be the underdog. The ones who belong to the underdogs are the ones cheering for Cedric, and that is the minority.

I once watched a video of sharks hunting an injured whale. The sharks get more and more excited every time another one of them goes in for an attack. That's a schoolyard fight. A feeding frenzy. A bunch of sharks hovering around, just waiting for the victim to grow weaker and weaker until they, too, can have a bite. And most times, the words kids throw around are what cause the worst wounds.

But sometimes, if the victim is lucky, the dolphins come to the rescue. This time, our dolphin appears in the form of Miss Yvette. There's relief as soon as there's an adult on the scene, and one who is not going to have any of this nonsense. She steps in, one arm out, keeping the other five Idiots from Russian Hill at bay. Her other hand yanks Ilya up by the collar of his blue coat. Cedric finally comes up for air and I see his face. Blood is seeping from his lip.

I snap my attention to Ilya. My tato was once talking to Ivan Markovych about a group of Russians he encountered who were harassing a group of Ukrainians in the park. Ultranationalists, he called them. Military expansionists spreading *Russkyi Mir*—the Russian world—he said. Ivan Markovych had one word that explained it all. *Rashist*—a term, he said, that is cooked up from the words *Russian, racist*, and *fascist*.

"You started this, Ilya Ilyich," I cry. "You stupid rash—!"

Before I can finish my insult, Miss Yvette is shaking me by the backpack and pulls me away.

"Mr. Chaban and Miss Len," she announces in English, "both of you to the director's office."

She turns to Cedric. Petro and Anna, two of our friends, are helping him up. "And you, Mr. Abara, you go to the nurse. Now," Miss Yvette stresses.

Then Miss Yvette frog-marches me and Ilya to the school building. The bell rings. The sharks pull away for calmer waters.

CHAPTER 3

Mom-*Мать*-*Мама*

Mr. Vovk is the new school director, having joined us right after Christmas. He introduced himself briefly at a class assembly and that was generally it. But Ilya and I are sitting outside his office, waiting to be disciplined, and I wonder if Mr. Vovk is going to be as terrifying as his predecessor, Mrs. Gregoriyeva. We were all scared of her. If you get kicked out of this school—one of the top in Ukraine—Tato says your future is going to be pretty slim. And she kicked out a lot of kids. I imagine a lot of them are now sleeping at the ferry docks or on benches around the train station.

Ilya is scuffing the parquet floor with his name-brand sneaker, making the wood squeak and the bench rock. He's chewing a piece of gum really loudly and I catch a whiff of pink chemicals. Bubblegum flavor.

I shift closer to the corner of my side and lean my head on my hand, digging the elbow into the walnut armrest. The door to the office opens and Miss Yvette waves us in.

Ilya pushes himself up with a sigh, like he's been through this a thousand times and it's just a routine nuisance. And I have to stop myself from laughing when my inner voice says, *The only routine nuisance here, Ilya, is you.*

When we squeeze by Miss Yvette, she says in English, "No funny business."

Mr. Vovk is behind his big, dark wood desk. He has bushy gray-black eyebrows that look like triangles without bottoms. His jowls hang a little over a wrinkly neck. He is tall—really tall—and is wearing a brown suit and blue necktie.

"Come in, you two," he says. He speaks in Russian to us. "Take a seat."

I lower my backpack to the floor and slump in the chair next to Ilya. Mr. Vovk folds his hands, like he's about to pray, and I hear Miss Yvette rustling behind us.

"What is the problem with you two?" Mr. Vovk says. "Why was there a fight?"

I look at Ilya, Ilya glances at me and shrugs. He owes me money. I owe him his homework. I am not going to be a tattletale if he isn't, so I sit back and fold my arms over my chest.

"Nothing happened," I say.

"Did you hit Cedric?" Mr. Vovk challenges.

"Me?" I say. "Hit Cedric? He's my best friend."

Mr. Vovk's triangles shoot up his forehead. He shakes his jowls and clears his throat. "So, Mr. Chaban, then it's you who punched Cedric."

"I don't know." Ilya shrugs again. "Did I?"

Mr. Vovk's face turns into a frown, and I think of Musty, Ivan Markovych's pit bull mix, whose face gets all wrinkly just before he starts to pant.

The director looks up at Miss Yvette, and he picks up the phone. "Whose mother should I call first?"

Ilya and I say the same thing at the same time—"I don't have a mom." Except Ilya calls his *Mat'*. I call mine *Mama*.

Mom-*Мать-Мама*. English-Russian-Ukrainian.

The room gets awfully quiet. Very slowly, Mr. Vovk lowers the phone back into the cradle.

"I'm sorry, I didn't know that. And your . . ."

Ilya shifts in his chair, leaning to his left. I copy him and lean to the right.

"We both have fathers," I say.

Mr. Vovk looks relieved. "Wait outside, you two."

Miss Yvette goes to her class and leaves us in the hallway. There we are again. Ilya and me. On that awful bench. I hear him make a popping sound. The chewing gum. It's something I doubt Major Chaban, Ilya's father, would approve of.

"Can I have one?" I ask.

Ilya squints at me first, whips that tuft of hair off his eye, then reaches into his coat pocket and produces a piece of Dirol.

I pop it into my mouth. "That really got him, huh?" I say. "When Mr. Vovk said he was going to call our mothers."

Ilya shrugs. "He's stupid. He doesn't know anything yet."

"That's not the same thing," I say.

"What's not the same thing?"

"Not knowing something doesn't mean you're stupid. It just means you don't know."

He scowls at me as if I've just said something outrageous.

I clear my throat. "I could give you your homework now. Do you have the money?"

He grumbles something, then gestures for me to open my bag and show him. I pull out the sketches and flip past Colin. It's the illustration that I plan to hand in but Ilya grabs the pad out of my hands.

"You drew a fish?"

"It's a dolphin," I huff. "That's Colin, from the dolphinarium. He's the oldest one. We've got four dolphins, and a Beluga whale and . . ."

He's turning the sketch around and I can tell he's impressed.

"It's a fish," he says.

"They're mammals, not fish."

"I forgot, Little Mermaid knows everything." He reaches into his pocket and waves a five-hryvnia bill in my face. "I'll take it."

I swallow hard and my gum goes down, leaving a slither of pink chemical taste in my throat. "Yours is on the next page. That one's mine. And we said twenty. Not five."

He rolls his eyes and flips the page, sees the gray kidney of Neptune, and scoffs. "I'm not handing that in. That's awful."

"But you can't draw, that's why."

He rips out the picture of Colin, making a big tear in the upper left-hand corner. My heart is hammering in my chest. He throws my sketch pad and the five hryvnia on my lap and they both slide to the floor, the sketchbook landing with a thud just as Mr. Vovk reappears.

"Ilya Ilyich, your father will be here in a moment." He looks to me just as I pick up the pad from the floor and hide the money beneath. "And Sofiya Oleksandrivna, yours said he will come right after he's done making Gummi drops for Roxi? Whatever that means."

"It means my tato is making gelatin cubes for our youngest dolphin. It's the only way she'll take her vitamins."

"Oh?" He scratches his head, then drops his arm to the side. "What class do you have this period?"

"English," I say.

"Then go on. Before you miss the whole lesson. Ilya Ilyich, your father wants you to wait here."

I see something interesting flash on Ilya's face as Mr. Vovk closes his door again. It's fear. But he quickly covers it up with that bored-with-this-routine expression.

"Give me my illustration. I have biology next period," I say.

Ilya groans. "Not my problem. I'm not handing in that stupid drawing you made."

"Ilya Ilyich Chaban, no teacher is going to believe you drew Colin. You're going to get us both into trouble."

On the opposite wall is a cabinet full of trophies. I jerk my head to a first-place fencing trophy where there is a photo of Ilya's father the year he won it for the school. Ilya's eyes dart to it, then back to me. Major Chaban is a no-nonsense kind of guy. My tato will take me home, have an overly long conversation with me, but Ilya's father? His dad is not the kind of man who *talks* to his kids.

"No funny business," I say in English. "Or I tell all."

Ilya's face flushes pink. "You wouldn't dare."

I stick my hand out. "I won't say a word. Not about who started the fight. Not about me doing your homework. Twenty more hryvnia for the drawing I made for you. Plus, for keeping my lips sealed."

Ilya stares at my hand, then looks up at me, grimacing like he's about to say, *No way.*

My hand is right beneath his nose. "Our fathers are coming, and if nothing was supposed to have happened in the schoolyard, then we better make it look like nothing happened. Besides, my name is on the back of the dolphin illustration already."

Ilya looks startled and pulls out the drawing from his bag. My name is penciled on the back. He reluctantly hands it over. It's not only torn now, it's wrinkled, too.

"What about Cedric?" he asks.

"He's with me. We stick together."

I carefully tear out the sketch of Neptune for him, and he squints at it.

"Actually, it's kind of good. But you made this line for 'tail' curved. Why?"

I smack my lips with impatience. "Because, Ilya, you always make mistakes." But I don't actually believe he is stupid. Lazy, maybe. Or worse yet, apathetic. Ilya simply doesn't care.

He scoots into his corner of the bench, and scowls again.

I hold out my hand once more. "Anyway, if I did it perfectly, the teacher would suspect. It's enough that I did the paw. You'll get extra credit. For extra money."

He lets out a small, surprised laugh. "I get it. Pretty clever." He gives me twenty more hryvnia. I don't move my hand. He sighs and reaches into his pocket again. Now I've got a total of thirty hryvnia from Ilya.

I make him shake my hand after I put the money away. As

I head down the corridor to English class, I pass by that trophy case with Major Chaban's fencing cup.

But behind the national chess trophy is a photo of my tato, Oleksandr Antonovych Len from when he was the chess champion. Ilya might take after his father's brawn, but I have inherited my father's strategic abilities.

CHAPTER 4

The Maidan

When I walk into English class, I'm surprised to find pictures hanging on the blackboard. There are photos of young, winter-clad men and women around bonfires in steel barrels. Big metal barricades, called hedgehogs, surround a lit-up pavilion. In another photo, the monuments of Kyiv, the Ukrainian capital, are all alight, but the sky above is pitch-dark. And there are young kids on their parents' shoulders, waving Ukrainian flags even though it has to be way past their bedtimes.

I recognize these images. We've seen them on TV and on the internet. They're the protesters who have occupied Maidan Square in Kyiv for nearly four months now. Now, when anyone talks about the Maidan, they talk about the revolution that has spread across Ukraine. From west to east, and north to south, every major city and even small villages hold their own "Maidans." Miss Yvette spent her entire Christmas vacation at Maidan Square in Kyiv, taking part in the protests. She saw the rock group Okean Elzy reunite there, and one of their songs has become the protest's anthem.

In a column to the right of the photos is a list of vocabulary words in white chalk. *Capital vs capitol. Protest. March. European Union. Free country. Borderland.* There's more, but Miss Yvette waves me to take a seat with Cedric and the rest of my group, which includes the twins Petro and Anna.

I already know the kind of activity they are doing. We have to read a short article, define the words, choose some of the pictures, and use the words to talk about the photos. They are big words for sixth form, but that's what makes Miss Yvette so cool. She makes us feel as if we *can* do these things. She says our job is to *want to* and her job is to make sure we are *able to*. 6A always *wants to*.

I'm not mad at Miss Yvette for breaking up the fight or bringing us to the director's office to be bawled out. I don't think Ilya resents her for it either, even though Major Chaban will likely ground him or something worse. We all genuinely like Miss Yvette.

Unlike any of the other teachers we have, she's a friend. What I like most about her is that she doesn't only teach us English. Miss Yvette brings in all kinds of interesting topics for us, like, what it's like to live in America, because she was born in Chicago and is Ukrainian American. Or, how in Turkey, she became a millionaire, earning a million Turkish lira a month, which was actually only a few hundred American dollars. That's also how she learned that the definition of wealth is relative. She told us about how she once mistook a tube of mayonnaise for toothpaste in a foreign country, too.

She came to Crimea to follow her grandparents' story and learn more about her family. When she arrived, she liked it so much, she decided to stay. And that's how we learned a lot about the Second World War and Ukraine's part in it. Not the Soviet Union's part, but Ukraine's. They don't even teach us that in history, she says. Not even later, when we're older.

Cedric shoves over his chair so that I can find some space at the table. He fist-bumps me. "How did it go? Big trouble?"

I shake my head. "It's just Ilya Ilyich, you know?"

Cedric nods and I see that he has a fat lip and some crusted blood where Ilya split it. I feel my anger rising again, but he smiles, touching it carefully. "It's not so bad."

I rub his shoulder, then look at what Anna is writing. "What's going on here?"

Though Petro and Anna are twins, they don't really look alike. Petro has brown hair and wears thin wire-framed glasses. Anna has long dark hair, thick and heavy like a curtain. Her bangs hang over bright blue eyes.

Petro pulls the sheet away from his sister in mid-sentence.

"Hey," she says. "I was working."

"Let Sofiya see," he says.

I read:

The Maidan revolution started because Ukrainians are angry that our president takes away our chance to join the European Union. It would make Ukraine one of the European states, like a new state in the United States. We would be a member of a very large, and very safe family.

A large and safe family. That would be nice.

I make a couple of corrections to the grammar.

"See?" Petro says to Anna. "I told you we had to use the past tense."

Anna's cheeks flush pink.

"We have to identify the different political parties," Cedric says, and points to a picture on the table with a group of adults on a stage.

"My tato has a lot to say about the politicians in Kyiv," Petro teases. "But I don't think that kind of vocabulary is on the board."

Cedric, Anna, and I giggle. Miss Yvette comes over, and I cover my mouth, still embarrassed about this morning.

"Everything okay?" she asks quietly.

"Yeah," I say.

She suddenly leans over our table, very serious, and speaks to us in Ukrainian. "Last night, things took a very big turn at Maidan Square," she says in a low voice. I wonder if, like last month, some protesters were shot at again, but instead, she says, "The president might be thrown out. If that happens, Ukraine has another chance to join the European Union."

"Another chance of becoming a state like in the U.S.?" Anna asks.

"Maybe," Miss Yvette confirms in English.

"My dad says our president is influenced by the Russian Federation," Petro says. "His orders are coming from the Russian government . . ."

"The Kremlin," I say. "Which is like the capitol—with an *o*—in Washington, DC. But for Russia."

Miss Yvette smiles at us and raises an eyebrow. "Now, tell me which of these parties are pro-European, and want Ukraine to become a part of the European Union?"

Anna and Petro start going at it. Cedric is really good at this because his father was a diplomat before he began teaching at the university. Plus, like me, Cedric's an only child, so we have to listen to a lot of adult talk.

"Sofiya, will you please come with me?" Miss Yvette suddenly says.

I follow her to the front of the room and I see a roll of tape on her desk.

"Ilya tore the illustration I have to hand in next period," I tell her quickly. "Can I have some?"

She waits until I come back with the sheet, and looks at it as I try to fix it, wrinkles and all.

"Did you draw that?" she asks.

I nod and she gently takes it out of my hand. "You're very talented."

"My mother was an artist . . ." I say. I'm surprised by the tears that burn in the back of my eyes. "But I'm going to be a veterinarian. Or a marine biologist."

Miss Yvette looks at me funnily. "There are a lot of different paths to get to where you want to go."

I don't know what she means, so I shrug.

"Your family and Ilya's family have a long history, don't you?" she asks.

I look away and shrug again.

"His mother, I mean. And your mother . . ."

I tense up at the mention of our mothers again, and Miss Yvette clicks her tongue.

"You were really young, I suppose," she says. "And it's really none of my business. Never mind. I shouldn't have said anything. I just wanted to check in on you and make sure you're okay."

She leaves me to finish taping Colin's torn tail. The tears are welling up. But they aren't for the rip that Ilya made. It's because I don't want to think about our mothers. His is gone because of a freak accident. But mine? It was her choice to leave us. I just wasn't enough to keep her here.

CHAPTER 5

My Family, the Pod

The day goes by, but I never end up getting called back to Mr. Vovk's office. So I do what I always do. I bike back to the waterfront and pull into the dolphinarium.

The main building is white and looks like a Greek temple with a terra-cotta roof. When the sun is straight up in the sky, the water turns berry blue. On winter afternoons, though, the sea is ice gray.

I lock my bike and take the entrance to the lowest level. Here, behind the glass, visitors can view the sea life beneath the water. The dolphinarium is built right on the harbor, but the animals are contained in artificial lagoons. They used to be held in pens in the Black Sea, but Tato decided that, because the harbor noise and pollution could make them sick, they should be moved into newly designed lagoons.

It's quiet down here. The air and sound are muted by the thick glass. It's dark, too, because the lights would confuse the animals. From here, I can watch what each dolphin and sea lion is doing in the lagoon.

The dolphins are up above, skimming the surface, playing

with their toys. They carry the balls in their beaks, then let go, and chase after them. Lily, with her scratched-up face, is swimming in circles with Roxi, like the two eager teenaged girls they are. Pesyk is making demands near the rim of the trainer stage. He's probably talking about how hungry he is. But it's Colin I'm waiting for, the oldest in the pod. He is nearly thirty years old, and the dolphinarium is planning a big birthday party in early May for him.

Tato was making plans for a big show for Colin. We wanted to do something extra special, but recently I've been overhearing conversations about funding and money. I'm not supposed to know about it, so I don't ask. All Tato says is that I shouldn't worry. But I do.

I recently suggested that we start a kids' camp over the school holidays.

"Kids helping kids," I said to Tato, though what I really meant was *kids helping the dolphinarium*. "The parents don't know what to do with their kids because most parents have to work," I said to him.

There's a Kids for Kids program at the community center that lets kids plan events and offers training in things they're good at. I suggested that we do that with students around the spring holidays, and teach them to work with the dolphins—how to do tricks, and so on. Then they could maybe help with the day's events for Colin's birthday.

Tato's eyes lit up and he scratched his forehead. "Kids helping kids. Huh. But how will we advertise it?"

"Social media!" I cried. "It's free! Plus, I can make posters and put them around the schools, ask my friends to take them to their sports clubs and music clubs."

Tato said he would think about it. I hope he says yes because I really want to celebrate Colin's birthday big.

Now, as I step up to the glass and look up, Colin suddenly dives down and hovers in front of me, suspended in the water. He nods his head, his black beady eye close to the glass.

Babushka once said that anytime we really look at someone in the eyes, we see two things: first a reflection of ourselves, and then the person we're looking at. And it's true. In Colin's eye, I first see myself in my furry white coat, my jeans and orange turtleneck. My eyes are green like olives. My hair is still a mess beneath my red cap. Colin whirs and clicks, then opens his mouth and goes *ah-ah-ah-ah*, as if he is scolding me because I didn't brush it properly. Then, I look beyond my reflection and I see only him. I know that Colin understands everything about me, and I understand everything about him.

I take the metal stairs that lead up to the top of the pools. Colin matches the angle of the staircase and glides as though he's going upward with me.

Upstairs, the five trainers who work for my tato are sorting out the fish buckets and organizing the equipment they use to train the dolphins. Each dolphin has their own bucket and will practice their tricks for food. I greet each trainer with a wave or a fist bump.

Colin has retrieved his ball, swims over to me, and tosses it onto the platform. I laugh, pick it up, and toss it back to him. Now, Roxi and Lily are fighting for attention, also tossing their balls at me. I find a bucket of ice cubes and slip a cube into each of their mouths. Colin, too. Pesyk is next.

In the summer season, the dolphinarium puts on shows for the tourists, but the rest of the year, groups of people in wheelchairs or on crutches or wearing prosthetics usually come in. Kids who have invisible disabilities come here, too. They swim with the dolphins, play with them, and learn about their habits. But we've been getting fewer calls and have seen fewer and fewer groups now that social funding keeps getting cut.

It's a waste, really. The marine mammals here are so smart. They understand people, just like Colin understands me. I like watching how the dolphins transform people from shy and uncertain to joyful and hopeful. Tato says people believe dolphins are mystical, spiritual creatures, but they aren't. They are complex mammals, with feelings and needs. They just happen to be really good-hearted.

Some kids have dogs and cats and hamsters as pets. Besides Neptune, I have four dolphins, two sea lions, and a rescued Beluga whale named Fizz.

That's where I find Tato. He's outside, washing down the platform near Fizz's huge training pool. Fizz pops up his big bubbly white head and nods at me.

When Tato spots me, he raises an eyebrow, calling over the noise of the hose. "I was at your school late this morning."

Uh-oh, I think.

"I made my acquaintance with your new director, Mr. Vovk."

I bite my lip.

"We need to talk."

"Okay." I sigh. I wonder how it's going for Ilya this afternoon.

Tato gestures for me to return to work, so I beeline it for the dolphin pod and try not to think about how upset he must be. From the buckets, I practice hand and whistle commands—turn my hand over so that the dolphins roll, or push my hand up and out so that Roxi, in this case, rises vertically onto her tail flukes and swims backward.

Tato is working with Roxi on a special experiment about dolphins and language and reporting his findings to a research center in Hawaii. Can they learn a whole language, and string sentences together? Solve problems? Communicate back? That's what he's been working on with Roxi. But not from gestures, or our facial expressions, but from *words*. Tato's enthusiasm began when I shared a YouTube story about a dog who can tell hundreds of toys apart by name alone.

Whether it's simple commands or more complicated experiments, we use positive reinforcement to reward the animals. In their case, with food and strokes. They also learn from one another. Cedric has a dog who has to work for his food, too. His father read a book that said feeding a dog from a bowl is like taking away a guitar from a musician: You effectively take away what they love doing best. In the dog's case, hunting for food. And in the dolphins' case, that's what we're doing, too. They have to work hard to get their fish because that's what they would have to do in the wild.

I toss fish to Roxi and Lily for following my commands, and they chirp excitedly.

"Great job, guys," I call to them. "*Klassno!*"

The dolphins love compliments, too. Who doesn't? They always look like they're smiling. Pesyk, which means "doggie," swims up next. He's only two years old and is light gray. He's Colin's companion male, because the older males love having someone younger in the pod.

"It's like taking your son and teaching him how to play ball," Tato once said. "Colin transfers all his knowledge over to

Pesyk, and shows him how to be the big shot in the pod."

Pesyk has a special bark when he talks and sometimes he emits low growls from his blowhole, which make him sound threatening, but I find him hilarious. Like a chihuahua who thinks he's a pit bull, except Pesyk really is a pretty big dolphin.

After he does a few spins, I toss him another fish. Colin is spy-hopping out of the water, where half his body is straight up over the surface, watching me. He stays like that, like a dog sitting on his hind legs begging. With my eyes, I tell Colin that I'm saving the biggest fish for him. I don't want to say I have a favorite, because I love them all. But Colin is special. We're able to talk to each other without words.

They are all part of my family. Just as I think this, there is that sadness again, that hole where Mama should be.

I make Colin jump through one of the hanging hoops, which he does with ease, and toss him the choice fish from his bucket last. The dolphins know feeding time is over when I tap the pails on the tile floor. They can break into fights sometimes, but they're peaceful today. Pesyk swims over to where my tato is nearly finished with Fizz at the opposite pool, probably hoping to get one last bite. Lily spy-hops and backs away, chirping as if to say, *Thank you*. Roxi swims past me and turns on her side, one fin and eye exposed just in case I have another snack for her. She's always hungry.

I reach forward and brush her as she swims by one more time.

"The fat lady has sung," I say to her. "Lights out now."

Colin suddenly surfaces where Roxi has left. I get on my knees and lay my hand on the edge. He places his beak there, or what we refer to as a rostrum. He makes a sound, almost like purring, but he's a dolphin, so it comes out of his blowhole like *trrrrr-trrrr-trrrrrr.*

Once, I asked Miss Yvette whether it was difficult for her to be so far away from home. I wanted her to say that she hated being away from her family. Instead, she said, "Home is where the heart is. This is my home now."

She didn't understand why I walked away so disappointed.

Colin suddenly nudges my arm.

"Hey!" I laugh.

But he chirps, and his eye is on me. When I place my hand on the rim of the pool, he quiets down and lays his rostrum on my hand. I say nothing. He says nothing. We don't need to. He and I just know what we know. Our hearts are here. This is our home. These dolphins are my family. And I always know that when I come here, Colin is waiting for me. I know he understands me.

"Sofiya," Tato calls. I know that tone. "I'll be in the office when you're finished."

That means I should get in there as soon as possible.

"Colin," I whisper, "I think I might be in trouble."

He raises his head away from mine and sinks back into the water, scolding me, like I'm not about to be reprimanded enough.

"I know, I know," I argue. "But Ilya was so mean!"

Colin is right, though. I need to control my temper better.

I drag my feet to Tato's office, only to discover that there is a second surprise today. A huge, unpleasant one. Just as I walk in, I see a black Mercedes sedan pull into the parking lot beyond the window. I know that vehicle. Major Chaban extracts himself from the driver's side. The passenger side opens up, too.

Ilya is here.

CHAPTER 6

Dad-*Отец*-*Тато*

What's going on?" I ask. There is panic in my voice.

Tato checks over his shoulder where Ilya and his father are walking toward the entrance of the building. "You and Ilya Ilyich Chaban are getting your sentences exacted."

"Sentences? What for?"

"For the fight today. Do you want to tell me what happened?"

"You mean besides Ilya being himself?"

Tato does that growly harrumph he makes when he knows he's not supposed to laugh but can't help it. "Yeah, besides that."

"He said something really racist to Cedric."

He tilts his head. "Got it. Regardless, you're going to help me with this. You're going to pretend that what I'm doing to *you* is a real chore."

I put my hands on my waist. "What is?"

"I convinced Mr. Vovk and Major Chaban that Ilya Ilyich should work here for a few weeks."

"No!" I groan. "Really? Here? But—"

"And you're going to help me."

I fall against the wall. "No, Tato. Please, please, please—"

"If you're going to do the dying swan dive," Tato says half joking, "can you do so more quietly? Don't you want to help?"

I stamp my foot. "Help you with what? With *what*?"

The door makes that whoosh-suck noise down the hall when someone opens it. Tato leans forward and points at some boxes. From the pictures, I see that they're cameras and other electronic equipment.

"Ilya might be able to help you with this idea of yours for the camp and Colin's birthday show. The hashtag Kids for Kids program."

"It's just Kids for Kids, Tato. You don't have to say hashtag for . . . oh, never mind."

"Maybe he's good with computers, or can design invitations."

"He can't draw!"

"Find out what he *can* do. We need a website for the camp. Registration pages. A way for them to make payments online. I thought you could put up some GoPro cameras around the pools and I don't know . . . vlog?"

"Vlog? What?"

"Create an Instagram account or on that new app, Telegraph."

"Telegram! It's called Telegram, Tato. But with *Ilya*?" My voice is hitting the teary stage. Then I eye the boxes and lift one of the cameras. They're a generic brand. Even so, maybe Tato is onto something, but . . . "With *Ilya,* Tato? For real?"

The marching steps make us both pause. Major Chaban orders one of the staff to tell him where my tato is.

"Sofiya, pretend like it's just another one of your chores," Tato whispers.

"A chore?" I protest. "That's *exactly* what it is with Ilya Chaban! Please, Tato, think of something else! Cedric is really good with computers. *He* could help me. Petro. Anna! They know their way around social media."

"Right," Tato says. "But Cedric didn't start the fight. You did. I found this to be a better alternative to . . ." He stops, and I know what he means. A better alternative to whatever Mr. Chaban dreams up for Ilya's punishment. "Besides, you can still ask your other friends to help. The more the merrier."

I can't really argue now that the dolphinarium is my escape from everything that goes wrong at school because Major Chaban and Ilya, both of whom are wearing permanent frowns, now come through the doorway.

Tato stands up, his hair long, his beard short. His T-shirt, stretched out and loose at the hips, is splattered with water.

Which is completely the opposite of how Major Chaban looks. Ilya's father is clean-shaven, has a round belly, two chins, and broad shoulders. His suit looks like a military uniform, it is so pristine.

I now know where Ilya has inherited his scowl.

Major Chaban does not look in the least bit happy about being here, but Ilya glances at me and I catch an expression of relief beneath that brown forelock when my tato pats his shoulder.

Tato then shakes the major's hand and speaks in Russian. "Welcome, Ilya Mikhailovich. Thank you for coming. It's been a . . . long time."

Tato again explains the plan he concocted with Mr. Vovk. "We're preparing for a big event here at the dolphinarium, and we have an idea for a youth program. I thought maybe our kids could work together on creating a lot of excitement and interest, visit other local schools about it, and so on. You know how kids are when they want something? Eventually, the parents give in. Besides, Ilya could maybe get to know the dolphins—"

Ilya gasps softly and takes a step back. His eyes are wide with fear. What's wrong with him? Every kid would love to be behind the scenes with the dolphins.

"I haven't agreed to this, Oleksandr Antonovych," Major

Chaban warns. He looks around the office, picks up one of the camera boxes. “I only agreed to discuss it with you. I’d like to see what you’ve done with the facilities since—”

“The animals are in for the night now.” Tato wraps his arms over his middle. It’s like he’s trying to hold himself back. “But I can show you around the foyer, some of the things we do. Sofiya? Coming?”

Tato’s reaction is odd, but I don’t say anything because I don’t want Ilya to be here anyway. And apparently, Tato doesn’t want Major Chaban to go to the lagoon either.

I linger behind them as Tato leads them out and Ilya suddenly falls in step with me. He doesn’t say anything and neither do I.

The foyer is filled with posters and cardboard cutouts of playful, cartoon dolphins and a Beluga whale, plus two sea lions. Ilya is not interested. He sulks, looking down at his shoes. He doesn’t even look at the photo collage that I helped the staff put together. They let me pick some of the photos. But Major Chaban is looking at them through squinted eyes. He peers really closely at a photo of a soldier who’d been in Afghanistan. In the photo, he is “hugging” Colin. Both of them are in the water and laughing, Colin with his head thrown back, the soldier, too. You can’t see that the man is missing his legs, but I know he is.

"So," the major says. "Colin is now a nurse and not a soldier."

I freeze. How does Ilya's father recognize Colin? Only a few people can tell the difference between the four dolphins, and I've never seen Major Chaban here.

"Yes," Tato says. "A lot has changed."

Changed? Changed since when?

"So I see." Major Chaban turns a little to where Ilya is standing and talks to him without really looking at him. "Your grandfather started that program, Ilya. He'd be . . . ashamed to see what the place has turned into."

Tato is still holding onto his middle. His chin drops to his chest and he clears his throat. "We help a lot of people here."

"It's nothing but a circus now," Ilya's father snaps. "We should never have demilitarized the place."

Tato suddenly looks at me as if he remembers that I'm there. His eyes dart to Ilya. To me, he speaks in Ukrainian. "Why don't you take Ilya to the underground?"

"But you said you didn't—"

"We'll be with you in a few minutes."

He means for me to leave. I look at Ilya and wave a hand at him, switching back to Russian. "Come on."

I lead him down the stairs and back the way I'd come in earlier this afternoon. It's dark. The water looks murky behind the glass of the sea pen, which is what happens when the tide comes in. Fish dart to and fro, but our animals are behind the lagoon glass.

Ilya is hanging out near the post, far away. I turn to him.

"Did you hand in the illustration?"

"Yeah." His eyes don't leave the lagoon. "But our teacher is suspicious."

"Did he say anything?"

Suddenly, Ilya releases a cry. I spin around just as one of the dolphins glides by.

"It's only Pesyk," I tell him. "He's our second male."

But Ilya has backpedaled to the exit doors. Just then, Tato pushes through, meaning to bring Major Chaban in as well. If Ilya were a cat, he'd have been on the ceiling, his claws dug deep into the Styrofoam tiles.

Major Chaban looks around him and something ripples over his face. "Very civilized. The whole installation . . ." He suddenly looks at Tato, then me, then at his son, and his expression turns sour.

"What's wrong with you, Ilya Ilyich? Are you scared of the dark, or what?"

Ilya shakes his head.

"Let's go, then. I've agreed to see how things develop. As long as this little project does not interrupt your studies . . ."

But Ilya is white-faced as he shakes his head. He looks as if this is the worst possible sentence he might ever get. I mean, I'm not happy about this at all, but Ilya is doubly so.

"Did you hear what I said?" Major Chaban suddenly barks. And he turns slowly around again, as if assessing both the sea pen and the lagoon before he orders, "Say good night, and let's go. You begin on Saturday."

Ilya swallows and mutters, *"Da, Otets."* Yes, Father.

"Okay, Sofiya?" Tato says in Ukrainian.

"Dobre, Tatu." Fine, Dad.

But nothing is fine. I want to know how Major Chaban knows my Colin.

CHAPTER 7

MMS

The next morning, at home, Tato is preparing almond milk in a blender, and I see the makings of bean burgers for dinner. I like bean burgers, especially when he tops them with guacamole.

I slam my schoolbag on the counter and Tato cocks an eyebrow at me.

"So," he says.

"So?" I watch him pour in the raw almonds.

"You'll get started with Ilya this weekend. I'm surprised how well that went, yesterday. I know it's a Saturday, but—"

"That's not what I'm worried about."

Tato doesn't pulse the blender. Instead, he pushes it aside. "You're angry?"

"Uh-huh."

"About what?"

"What did Major Chaban mean when he said Colin is a nurse and not a soldier now? And all that other stuff about Ilya's grandfather . . . ? How does he know Colin?"

Tato does this thing where he takes in a breath and holds it.

Not like when he does yoga, but like when he has to force himself to keep from saying the first thing that comes to mind.

"Colin was not always a therapy dolphin. And Fizz was not really a rescue animal, per se."

"What are you talking about?" I whip off my beanie and put my hands on my hips. "Then what were they?"

"They used to be MMS. Military marine systems."

"Military marine systems? What is that?" I splutter. I remember the penguins from *Madagascar* and start laughing. "Wait? For real?"

It's an expression Miss Yvette always says when she's surprised: *for real?*

"For real," Tato says. "The sea lions were MMS, too."

"How can sea lions and dolphins and whales work for the military?"

Tato takes another breath before he explains. "Colin was trained to patrol the waters. For example, if enemy divers came near the navy yards to sabotage or damage the ships, he was like a guard dog. The Soviets trained the dolphins the way we train them now, except for different purposes. In addition to many other skills, dolphins can detect mines."

"With their built-in sonar systems," I say. "Echolocation."

Tato wags his finger in a way that means, *exactly*. But I don't like the picture I'm getting. And why hasn't Tato ever told me this before?

"And the sea lions and Beluga whales can be used as spies," he says. "Following ships. Planting mines on the seafloor." He places the blender between us again, turns it on, and shouts over the noise. "They carry cameras and follow foreign vessels. Fizz escaped from the dolphinarium, though. Twice. He crossed the Black Sea and was found in Turkey. The locals loved him, and even named him Aydin. He was chipped, though, and Fizz was returned to us. Belugas and sea lions. They're good in the Arctic waters, where the Russians have a lot of interests as well."

I wait until he's done and he pours us each a glass. He adds a touch of honey to mine, like an apology. I'm ready for the almond milk, not so ready for the apology. I suddenly see my English book still on the coffee table. I hurry to grab it and recall Miss Yvette's discussions about the Maidan and about our Ukrainian president.

"The Russians are interested in Ukraine," I say. "In the Crimean Peninsula, and the Arctic. Is there any place that the Russians are not interested in?"

My tato turns to the sink and rinses out the blender. "Very good question, Sofiya," he mutters.

"So, does Colin still remember how to soldier?" I ask when he's finished. I wince at the thought of Colin having an entirely different life, a dangerous life, before I even knew him.

"I suppose so."

He's drying the blender, and I swing my rucksack onto my back. I'm going to be late if I don't leave soon.

"Did he ever get hurt on the job?" I'm afraid to know the answer.

Tato looks at the clock, too. "That's a question for Babushka. She was their veterinarian back in the day. She's coming Saturday afternoon. You can ask her then."

At the mention of Babushka, I am both surprised and softened. She knows everything. I write all her stories down in my observation journal. But right now, I have no idea whether to be excited to see Babushka or irritated that my animals were used for warfare.

Tato shoves me out the door, and even though I know I'm late, I stop at the Monument to the Sunken Ships and scan the waters. It's weird. There are more navy ships out on the horizon than usual. The Russian navy leases Ukraine's port in Sevastopol, but they aren't usually very active. They are today. There are two heading for the harbor, and several other smaller patrol boats are out there, too. I imagine our marine mammals with them, finding dangerous mines, or having to stop threatening spies. I imagine Ilya's grandfather, an older version of Major Chaban, commanding them.

I don't like the idea one bit.

CHAPTER 8

Reward and Punishment

I'm rolling a cart of fish to the holding area early on Saturday morning as I hear the staff door open. We're still closed to the public for a couple of hours, and nearly everyone else who needs to be here is already here. The footsteps get louder and louder in the dark hallway.

Instinctively, I duck into the storage room, where Tato has put all the cameras and boxes next to the colored paper. As if to give me away, the copying machine suddenly starts up. It pants and wheezes in the corner.

"Hello?"

It's Ilya's voice.

I roll my eyes and step out of hiding before it becomes embarrassing. "I'm here."

"Oh." He is wearing his blue spacesuit jacket and a backpack. His boots are shiny from melting snow. He smells of rain.

"You can put your stuff over there." I point to the locker room for the employees. "I'll be in the kitchen. Come there when you're done."

He shuffles into the room, and there is a metallic clang

from one of the lockers before he reappears in the kitchen.

"This is so stupid. Who throws a party for a dolphin?" he complains.

"We do," I say.

I pull open the freezer and withdraw tubs of fish on ice. Ilya wrinkles his nose.

"It smells like fish," he complains.

"That's because it is. This is where we prepare the food." I roll my eyes when my back is to him again.

I check the mackerel and the five other varieties of fish we feed to the dolphins. They can't be broken in any way and can't have any cuts, which could take on bacteria. When I've sorted them out, I put them into a big bucket and fill it with water.

"I thought we had to make a website or something," Ilya mumbles. "Not work in a zoo."

I haven't even asked him to do anything, but I've got chores. And he's getting in the way.

"What are you doing?" He points to the bucket of fish and water.

"We have to prepare the food for each of the dolphins." I sound very official, like my tato does when he conducts tours. "We put the fish in water again so that they can take in the fluids. When they freeze, the fluids decrease, and since dolphins don't drink water—"

"What?" Ilya grimaces again, and shakes his head. "Why wouldn't they? They're *in* the water."

"Because they don't," I say over my shoulder. "Would *you* drink the water out of your bathtub?"

Ilya snorts.

I turn off the tap and show him the contents. "They get their fluids from the fresh fish they eat. That's why we put the fluids back in."

I set the buckets on the cart and shove it to him so that the handles are facing him. "Follow me."

I don't check to see if he does as I go into the next room, where there is a metal table with a row of stainless steel pails, one for each animal. I check the magnetic board and, out of the corner of my eye, I see that Ilya is in the doorway.

"The food is all portioned out here," I say. I point to the chart pinned above me. "Here's how much each dolphin gets, and how many vitamins. They get extra vitamins because they don't get everything they need just from the fish."

Ilya has abandoned the wheeled cart and is leaning, arms folded, against the cold metal counter where the sink is. He's not really paying attention. He looks at the clock. It's a long time before he can go back home, but it *is* time to put him in his place.

I open the mini refrigerator and pull out the vitamins for

Colin. I go to the nearest bucket of mackerel, hold one up, take a pill and open up the dead fish's mouth, then stuff the vitamin in, before dropping it into Colin's metal bucket.

I extend the next pill and a wobbly mackerel to Ilya. "Now you."

Ilya scowls. "I'm not here to be your assistant. This is not what I came here for."

"First the animals, then the fun," I say, just like Tato. "Go on. Stuff the vitamin in." I wiggle the fish over at Ilya and he backs away, turns around, and storms out.

Tetyana, one of the trainers who let Ilya in, walks in and looks at me. "Sofiya, don't you think you're being too hard on him?"

"Why?" I said. "He's here to work, isn't he?"

She nods with a half smile. "Go on. I'll take care of the portioning."

I find Ilya standing in the foyer. He's now looking at the photo collage.

"What's wrong with all these kids?" he asks, like it's a personal affront.

"They have Down syndrome."

"How does this one in a wheelchair even get into the water?" He points at Felix, a quadriplegic who used to come here every four weeks and work with Lily.

"We have special harnesses for him. Come on. I'll show you

where we work," I say. Only because I want to go to the dolphins.

I head for the pools but I don't hear him following me, so I look over my shoulder. Ilya is lingering uncertainly next to the cardboard cutouts of cartoon dolphins.

"Don't you want to meet the pod?"

His mouth twitches.

"Come on, you chicken."

"I'm not chicken."

"Then let's go."

He moves and I open the door. The animal smell and bleach hit me in the face. I'm not bothered by the smell anymore, but I can imagine what Ilya is feeling and seeing, hearing and smelling. The floors have been wiped down. The walls are made of blue and white tiles. We're in the inside pools, where it's warm and humid. The animals come through the underwater gates between here and the heated lagoon. There are two rooms and two pools, separated by a door. In the other room, the two sea lions bark their greetings, echoes bouncing all over the walls. The smell of fish is stronger here.

In the next pool, I spot Fizz in the water first. Then the four gray shapes of my dolphins appear. They raise their heads and start their chatter. They're louder than the sea lions now.

"Say, hi," I call to Ilya. "This is the morning concert."

I return to where Ilya is standing between the two doorways, like he's trapped. He throws a look at the sea lions, then at the dolphins. I ignore him and kneel down on the platform. Colin comes by, but when he turns on his side and shows his flipper, his eye is on something behind me.

Ilya is still where he was.

"It stinks in here," he shouts over the noise.

"Have you *never* been to a zoo?

"What do you do with all their poop?" he mocks.

"Well, Ilya," I say, and stand up, my hands on my hips. "The same as when *you* poop in a swimming pool. It's called a filtration system."

"I don't—" he starts angrily. There's the sound of a lot of water, and he steps over the threshold and backs into the sea lions' area, his eyes wide.

I turn to the pool. Colin has raised himself vertically and is propelling himself backward on his tail fin. Tato calls this move the "boogie-woogie."

A few meters later, Colin dives backward into the water, then swims back over to the rim of the pool. He turns over onto his back, both flippers up as he passes by.

"Come on," I say to Ilya. "He wants to meet you. You can stroke him."

Ilya doesn't move. His hands are gripped together in front of him. I wave him over.

Colin comes up chirping and whirring.

"Now, you listen here," I scold Colin, but I'm smiling as I do. "You're going to play nice with Ilya today."

"You can't talk to dolphins," Ilya calls from his spot of safety.

"What are you talking about? Of course I can."

"Right. So, what's he saying?"

Colin's eye is still on Ilya. But Pesyk, Lily, and Roxi now pop up and become demanding. Food's supposed to be coming.

"He's saying it's okay," I call. "You can come over."

Behind Ilya, I hear a deep *argh-argh-argh-argh!* as the biggest sea lion slaps his way over. I laugh, because I know what's going on, and then it happens. The sea lion curves his neck and begins his charge, straight for Ilya. Ilya turns away just in time, and stumbles into the dolphin area. I spring up and come between him and the sea lion.

I scold the animal in Ukrainian. He stretches his neck and presses his head up against the doorjamb, whiskers twitching and eyes rolling sideways.

"Go on," I say more gently to him.

The sea lion talks back but rushes toward his pool and slides in with a loud splash.

Ilya is now really lost. He's up against the wall, and the dolphins and Fizz are still swimming around peacefully but keeping their eye out for the rest of the trainers and the buckets of fish. Ilya must think they're keeping their eyes on him.

"You were saying?" I add as I pass by. "About not being able to communicate with the animals?"

To his credit, he does not respond.

"They're like dogs," I say. "They know what we want from them."

Ilya shakes his head, like he doesn't understand.

"It's just like training a dog," I explain.

Tetyana comes with the cart of fish. Two other trainers head in with a bucket each. I rush over and grab Colin's portion, and nod at Tetyana to let her know I'll work with Colin. I fish out my whistle from inside my shirt pocket and hang it around my neck before returning to the staging area.

Ilya has taken a step, maybe one and a half, in the direction of the pool.

"Come closer," I call over my shoulder. "So you can see."

The trainers and I check on one another before we start. Each one calls their dolphin with their whistle blasts. Each one has their own name. I start explaining just as Tato does when he's showing the visitors.

"Dolphins are hunters, so we don't just bend down and give

them fish. They have to work for their food. They have to make an effort." I turn my hand and Colin rolls over, then returns. I give him one of the vitamin-filled mackerels first. He opens his beak and I slide it in. I hear Ilya behind me make a noise, like a whimper. But he's come closer.

I continue. "But it's not any trick. They have to do what I tell them or they don't get their food."

The trainers all look at one another. I make a hand signal for Colin to slap his tail in the water. I don't do that often, because it can be seen as aggressive by the rest of the pod or a sign of warning, *Danger!*, which is why all the trainers do it together like we do in the shows. Now I'm free to do what I want with Colin. I feed him another mackerel first.

"How do you teach them to do tricks?" Ilya asks.

I have to turn around because I'm surprised. Ilya's not asking meanly. He's genuinely interested.

"When they're young," I start, "we reward them for the behavior we want. If they are acting up or aren't doing what we hope for them to do, then they don't get their fish. It's a lot of waiting and watching and then being quick about rewarding them. If they get sassy and shovel water at you, they don't get rewarded. But if they jump out of the water . . ."

I signal Colin to leap out of the water. He swims around to the back, then heads for me and springs into the air before landing in the water again and surfacing where I am.

I reach over into the bucket of fish and give one to Colin. "See? Then there's a reward. And when one of the other trainers wants to do a big job, Colin has to stay by me. He's being quiet now, just waiting. So I reward him." I drop another fish into his beak. "He thinks that if he keeps doing this, he'll get another fish."

Ilya loosens his hands and drops them to his side. "I don't get it. You have to *wait* until they behave correctly? Why don't you train them by punishing them when they don't do what you want them to do?"

I signal Colin again and he submerges and dives deep down toward one of the rubber rings at the bottom of the pool.

I frown at Ilya. "Punish them? Is that how your grandfather trained Colin before? By punishing him? No, Ilya, it's positive reinforcement that is more effective. Otherwise, the animals get scared of you. That's no basis for building trust."

"Trust? Who is talking about trust?" He sneers. "You should want them to respect you."

I can't help but look at Colin now and think of what he might have gone through as a military marine mammal. All I want to do is get in the water and protect him now, but something happens.

Colin has returned and he tosses the red ring. It skids to a stop at Ilya's feet. We eye each other for a second before I snatch it up and toss it back to Colin, who goes after it.

I turn to Ilya. Now I'm glad that he's not coming anywhere near Colin. "What's better? Respect or love?" I demand.

Ilya's face scrunches up and he folds his arms in front of himself. He shrugs.

Colin comes back and tosses the ring once more. This time, I have to maneuver toward Ilya and I catch it in my hand. What is Colin doing throwing this ring to this kid? I toss Colin a fish for bringing back the ring.

"Gentle," I say. I kneel down and pat the rim so that Colin knows to keep his rostrum there. He chirps and whirs softly.

From the corner of my eye, I see Ilya shift over so he can see. I look at him. Something has changed on his face. I look at Colin, who is also very interested. He suddenly backs up and nods, begging for the ring. He really does want Ilya to toss it.

Sighing, I extend the toy to Ilya. "He wants you to try."

Ilya shakes his head.

"Come on. It's like playing fetch with a dog."

"I never had a dog."

"Just throw it in already!" I get up and stride over to him. "You don't even have to get closer. He wants to play catch with you."

Ilya reaches for the ring, but just then Colin makes a

cackling sound through his blowhole. Ilya snaps back his hand, and I lunge and grab it in mine.

"Take the stupid ring!"

"Let go," he cries.

"Ilya Ilyich," I say, sounding like him when he's mocking someone. "You're the only person in the world who has never wanted to touch or play with a dolphin. What is wrong with you?"

"What's wrong with *you*?" He is indignant.

"Nothing's wrong with me," I shout. I throw the ring into the water but stare Ilya down. "I'm not the one who has to pay someone to do their homework."

Behind me, I hear the door bang shut, but Ilya pushes up against me and is looking down at me. He's got green specks in his eyes.

"Well, if you had just given me the dolphin drawing instead of that stupid cat you drew, I would've gotten a better grade."

"Ha! You're lucky I didn't charge you *fifty* hryvnia for my cat!"

"What's going on here?"

Ilya and I pull apart as if electrocuted. Tato is standing near the door, his arms crossed, his feet planted wide. "What are you two talking about?"

"Nothing," I say.

Ilya is stone silent. Like his lips have been superglued together.

"Nothing?" Tato looks at Ilya. Then back at me. "You're doing his homework for him? For *money*?"

My eyes dart to Ilya. He's scuffs his shoe against the blue-and-white tiled floor.

"Actually, Sofiya," Tato says in his half-hurt, half-angry tone, "you don't have to say anything. I heard it all. So spare yourself the stories. All I can say is that I am disappointed. *Really* disappointed."

Tato then points to the pool. "While you two are fighting, who's feeding and training Colin?"

I hang my head.

Tato's tone is still filled with irritation. "Sorry, Ilya. I know you just got here, but your father called. He wants you home as soon as possible. He said you can come back tomorrow. Maybe by then"—he looks at me again—"we'll all be in a more accommodating mood."

Ilya looks thrilled to be leaving, and starts heading to the exit door. Just then, Colin throws himself onto the rim, chattering and whirring. The red rubber ring flies through the air and lands near Ilya's feet. Ilya stops and stares at it. Colin rises up and spy-hops backward, waving one fin.

Ilya reaches down and takes the ring. He's thinking. Then he takes a couple of steps toward the pool and tosses the ring in.

Tato smiles at Ilya. "Looks like Colin's got you trained."

I look at Colin coming back up with the ring and then at Ilya. At me, Ilya frowns, but just before he leaves, Colin tosses the ring back at him. This time, Ilya walks over, picks it up, and tosses it in again. He looks at Tato, and I catch a flicker of a smile.

"Good job," Tato says. He pats Ilya's shoulder as he passes by. He then turns to me, and his face switches back to dark disappointment. "Get back to work, Sofiya."

CHAPTER 9

The Hole in Our Wall

I'm grounded. House arrest.

Our house on Vul. Rybochka looks like any house from the outside. It probably needs a new coat of yellow paint, but the red shutters are still bright. There is a small yard, and a bay window that Tato built in at the front.

Inside, between the kitchen and the living room, there is a big hole on the pale green wall.

The wall itself doesn't have a single dent. It is smooth and even, except for the small holes where the nails once were. "The hole" is what I call the empty space where my parents' wedding photos and our family photos used to hang.

It's been a hole since my mother's postcard arrived from Moscow. Not a postcard *of* Moscow; it was not a picture of Red Square, or the Kremlin, or Saint Basil's Cathedral. The postcard was of Sevastopol Bay. It had the Monument to the Sunken Ships jutting out of the water. Our blue-and-yellow flag unfurled over the sea.

My mother must have bought it at Ivan's food truck before she boarded the bus for Russia three years ago. I wonder if she already knew what she was going to write when she bought it.

To work off my anger, I pull out my sketchbook. It's not about being grounded. When Tato's right, he's right. I know I did wrong. But he just can't understand *why* I did Ilya's homework. He keeps telling me I have to be happy with the things I have, that there are certain things worth fighting for and other things you just have to let go.

So? What? He let go of my mother?

And *then* he actually looked at Ilya as if he was *proud* of him. The kid whose grandfather punished our dolphins to do what he wanted them to do. And for what? Why was my tato so pleased with Ilya? For throwing a stupid ring into the water? I'm the one who got him to get that close in the first place!

I start drawing. I have no plan. I just let the picture materialize. When I'm done, I stare at it and slowly rip it out of the sketchbook. I find the masking tape in Tato's utility drawer, which I'm not supposed to go into, and grab the stepladder from between the refrigerator and the wall. I reach on tiptoe into the highest kitchen cabinet. There, way in the back, is that postcard.

I stick both the illustration and the postcard over "the hole" on the green wall. My mother's handwriting is there for the whole world to see:

Я больше не вернусь.

I'm not coming back.

Neptune is snoozing in the bay window, his paw twitching on occasion, as if he's trying to shake off a fly. I adjust the sketchbook on my knees and decide I can do better than what I'd done for Ilya.

"It's nearly *purrfect*." I hold it up for Neptune to see.

He opens his eyes wide and gazes at the illustration of his paw, then shuts them again and starts up his motor.

I am labeling the different parts when Babushka walks through the front door. She puts two grocery bags down and takes off her coat before peering over my shoulder.

"That's quite good," she says.

I close the sketchbook and give her three quick kisses on the cheeks, then follow her into the kitchen and rummage through the grocery bags. She's brought extra pickles from her cellar. I take one glass jar out and shake it like a snow globe. The pieces of dill and garlic and mustard seed swirl around in a sea of vinegar.

She's got that twitchy smile she gives me when I'm enjoying her food. "Go ahead," she invites.

I pop the canning lid open and inhale. It smells like summer. Babushka makes the best pickles in the whole world.

Really, the whole world. I take two, one to devour and one to savor.

"Your father is out helping Ivan Markovych with the truck," she says. "He'll be back in time for dinner."

I wait. If Tato has told her about me and Ilya, she's probably going to lecture me, too.

But she doesn't.

She's on her way into the living room when she stops at the hole in the wall. I take the second pickle out of my mouth and watch her examining my sketch.

"What is this?" she finally says.

She knows what it is because I've labeled it. It's a drawing of my mother on a bus to Moscow from a bird's-eye view. The roof of the bus is gone, revealing the empty seats except one. In that one space is the top of my mother's head, her elbows jutting out from folded arms. Her long legs are in the aisles. She's wearing sandals, because she left in the summertime.

All around the bus, I've labeled the parts: *steering wheel, wheels, driver, rearview mirror, window . . . Mama.*

My mother is facing the front of the bus. I'm standing on the road, behind it. The bird's-eye view of me is just the top of my head and shoulders. My hair is a mess, like it's made of Medusa's snakes.

Babushka has turned to me. She's waiting for an answer.

"I just felt like drawing it."

"And hanging it up?" She points at the wall. "Here?"

I shrug and bite down on the second pickle. "I'll take it down before he comes home."

Again the sigh, but this time her mouth is one thin line. "What happened?"

So, Tato definitely did not tell her.

I finish the pickle, drift to the sofa, and wrap the wool throw around me like a toga. It is chilly in the house.

"You want to know what happened?" I ask Babushka. "Major Chaban was at the dolphinarium with Ilya, and I heard him say that Colin was a soldier, not a nurse."

Babushka straightens up tall, like someone just stuck a rod down her back. My grandmother is not a gray-haired woman wearing a scarf on her head. Her hair has white streaks but it's mostly still dark brown. Her hands are long and slender, and I can see the veins, but they're strong hands. She is wise and commands respect. Everyone we meet calls her "Dr. Len" or "*Pani Doktorova.*"

She sits down on the smaller sofa, the one covered with a kilim, and folds her hands in her lap. The glass coffee table is between us. "So, you heard about the military training program? What did Tato tell you?"

I lean forward, and my blanket-toga slips off my shoulder. "Tato didn't say much, but Ilya has a bad outlook on how to treat animals and getting them to do what you want them to do."

Babushka huffs and nods, but doesn't smile. "Just like his grandfather. Just like his father."

"Tato also said that you were the animal doctor for them, too."

"In Soviet times, yes. And for a while after the Ukrainians took the pods over and privatized the dolphinarium. Your father was young, your age, when he used to come with me to the dolphinarium. It was a training center then."

"Tato said the dolphins can be used as spies."

"Yes, or to prevent enemy divers from coming into the navy shipyards and planting explosives on the boats. Stealing secrets, or whatever it is that enemies do to enemies."

"And that sea lions and whales, like Fizz, are used for up in the Arctic."

"Placing mines, detecting mines, following ships and boats. All of it," Babushka says.

"Ilya hates the dolphins. I think he hates all animals."

"Ilya? Ilya Chaban? Why was he even there today?"

I shrug. I don't want to tell her what I did. I'll leave that up to Tato when he comes home.

Babushka frowns a little and clicks her tongue. She stands

up and returns to the kitchen. "Hate is a strong word, *kotyku.* After what happened to him and his mother—"

"Do you remember Ilya's mother?" I call to her.

"Of course I do," she says. "Don't you?"

"Why would I?"

"Because you were there."

I pause. I don't know what she's talking about.

"You were both there," she insists. "You and Ilya. The day of the accident."

"How old were we?"

"Maybe three. Four? You were all on the same boat."

This surprises me a lot. "I don't remember."

Babushka tugs at the ends of her hip-length cardigan. "I don't think Ilya hates the dolphins. I think he's terrified of them."

I shake my head. "What kid is terrified of dolphins?"

"Major Chaban never believed his son should receive help for what happened to him," she mutters.

"What happened? Why would he need help?"

She sits down and taps the fake gold rim of the coffee table with her foot. "Because he is still traumatized. By the water. By the waves. By the dolphins."

I suddenly get a picture of Ilya last summer, sitting on the concrete landing of the promenade while everyone else is down on the water, climbing around the rocks, laughing at the sea spray as it shoots up from the crashing waves. It hits me then.

"He's afraid to swim?"

But Babushka shakes her head. "I believe he is afraid of dying."

She then tells me the story, about the vacation in the southeast part of the peninsula, and how Ilya's parents, and my mother and I, were all on a boat.

"The sea became very stormy, so Major Chaban began racing to get back to shore. A pod of Black Sea bottlenose dolphins was following the boat."

As she continues, I can picture a younger version of Ilya laughing at the way the dolphins chased after us and how he started reaching out over the boat, farther and farther. There are other images, but out of focus: a woman with full lips and dark brown hair, my mother laughing and leaning into her. *Elena.* That was Ilya's mother's name.

I'm not so sure I want to remember any more.

"There was a lot of spray, a lot of waves," Babushka says. "Then the dolphins disappeared and Ilya wanted them to come back."

Babushka pauses. "Don't you remember any of this?"

I shake my head. Why should I?

After a moment, she says, "The boat was going at top speed. Ilya fell overboard."

My mouth drops open.

"Ilya was in the water, with a life jacket, thank God. But . . . well, Elena—his mother—jumped in after him. There was a large wave that crashed over her. They searched and searched, but no one could find her after that. Ilya was the only one who was saved."

Tears spring into my eyes and I wipe them away, then play with the fringes of the blanket. "I was really mean to him today."

"Because you didn't understand. To understand, Sofiya, you must ask the right questions." Babushka looks behind her, at my picture on the wall. "So let me ask you one."

I pull my knees to my chest and wrap the blanket tighter around me. I don't say anything because her question will come whether I want it to or not.

"Do you blame yourself for your mother leaving?"

I rest my chin on my knees and look past her, to Neptune in the window, who opens his eyes at that moment and stares right back.

"*Solodku . . . kotyku*," Babushka says softly. It's what she calls me: *Sweetheart. Kitten.* "It's not your fault. You know that, don't you? How many times does your tato . . . how many times do *I* have to tell you that?"

Neptune stands up, arches his back and stretches, then sits and faces me.

"I did not know my father, Sofiya."

"You didn't?"

"Your great-grandfather was one of the thousands of Crimean Tatars who was deported when the Russians cleared the peninsula. This was during the war."

She means the Second World War. I rest my elbows on my thighs, chin in my hands. "Where did they send him?"

"To Siberia."

I throw myself back against the sofa. "That may be, but nobody sent my mother away. She left on her own."

Babushka's folded hands bounce with her knees. She is looking at me but I can't look her in the eye. She waits. When I finally do, uncomfortable in the silence, she tilts her head.

"Some people don't need to be deported to feel like they've been forced out of their homes, Sofiya. Sometimes, for some people, it can feel like your own mind has turned on you and forced you out."

She stands up and pats my leg. I watch her go into the kitchen.

"Babushka? Why was I there? The day Ilya's mother drowned?"

She turns to me and frowns. "You really don't remember, do you? Ilya's mother and your mother were best friends. You and Ilya were inseparable."

"Best friends?" I wonder aloud. And I suddenly remember something else. Ilya's mother had been half Ukrainian. So that would make Ilya and me almost both half-and-half. But before I can confirm this, Babushka says something that breaks my heart more than it's ever been.

"Kotyku, it was your mother who was holding Ilya before he fell overboard. Even though he was rescued, she never forgave herself for her friend's death, Sofiya. How can a person who hates herself love anyone else?"

CHAPTER 10

The President Runs Away from Home, Too

Sundays are kind of our family day. Sometimes, when the weather is nice, Tato takes me to Ivan Markovych's food truck and we sit outside with the three pit bulls, Musty, Monk, and Marble, and play board games. Tato and Ivan always have a chess game going on the side, and in between serving his customers, Ivan steps out to watch Tato deliberate his next move, or to consider his own. Often, the customers have to wait a long time, but they are patient and watch the game in silence.

If it's raining or too cold, Tato makes a large egg breakfast and we play backgammon or Yahtzee at home. Sometimes, Neptune will jump up on the coffee table and push a die or game piece around.

But on this Sunday, I'm supposed to meet Ilya at the dolphinarium. This is my punishment. Instead of spending the day with Tato, I have to pay my dues. And now that I know about Ilya's traumatic experience—the fact that his mother and my mother were best friends, that I was on that boat when his mother drowned—I'm even more confused about him than before.

Out in the living room, Tato is nowhere to be found. But there is a note.

Meet me at the food truck first.

He hadn't come home until long after I'd gone to bed. I heard him and Babushka talking in low tones. I figured it was about me, and now I don't know if I'm in trouble again.

The note is next to the desk calendar and I tear off yesterday's date. The top sheet now says Sunday, February 23. I am just about to head out when Babushka suddenly appears at the garden gate. She's all bundled up. Her brow is furrowed.

"Where's your tato?"

"At the food truck?"

"Did he hear the news?"

"What news?"

She opens her mouth, then closes it. Her lips are pressed so firmly together that I can see the whites around them. "I'll come with you," she finally says, although she's already bustled me out the gate.

We walk to the promenade, which takes twenty-five minutes. The sky is clouded over and the temperature has to be below zero. I can barely see Babushka's lower face, tucked deep into the collar of her coat. But something is flashing in her eyes, and it scares me. We don't speak.

From the pavement, I can see that a crowd has gathered around Ivan's food truck. The dogs are sniffing around. When Marble sees me, he lopes over, his tail wagging. Musty and Monk follow him and surround me, nudging and protective. I look through the crowd to find Tato and see that Ivan Markovych is outside the truck. He's not cooking. I don't recognize most of the men gathered here. They are wearing caps with earflaps pulled tight against their heads, or scarves over half their faces. But there is a lot of noise here. Everyone is talking over one another, in Russian, in Ukrainian, and even in Crimean Tartar.

I find Tato, and expect him to pick up where we left off with Ilya and the homework, and the dolphins and all of that. But he puts a hand on my head and steers me closer to him.

"What happened?" I ask him.

"President Yanukovych has fled the country," he says. I can sense that he's worried. "Are you hungry?"

I was when I got up, but I'm not anymore, so I shake my head. "What does it mean, he fled?"

"It means Ukraine doesn't have anyone leading the country. It leaves us vulnerable, Sofiya. It leaves us vulnerable to Russia and Putin."

Vladimir Vladimirovich Putin. The Russian president's name is like a swear word among some here in Sevastopol.

Ivan and my father call themselves Ukrainian patriots, as do a lot of other people who hang out at the food truck. They claim that Putin wants to take us back to the Soviet era. The Ukrainian and Tatar populations are pretty small in comparison to the Russian population around here. And it's no secret that a lot of the Russians here love Vladimir Putin.

Ivan Markovych moves back behind the serving window. Behind me, the sounds of people arguing get louder. A group of men and women stop in front of us.

"Your corrupt people in Kyiv did this," a man next to me suddenly accuses our crowd. He's speaking Russian. "But it will be Putin who saves you. It's time Crimea is back under the Russian Federation."

"Who are you talking to?" Ivan shouts at the man in Ukrainian. But he switches to Russian. "You want the Russian Federation? Go back to Russia! Ukraine has been free of you since 1991! Crimea's been autonomous ever since!"

Others in the crowd grumble at the man, too. "Get out of here. Get your food elsewhere!"

Ivan steps out of the food truck now and confronts them, his chest expanding. I watch him from a distance. Ivan is from the mainland of Ukraine, near Zaporizhzhia. If I drew him from top to bottom, I'd have to start with an egg head, and then a triangular torso, thin hips, and muscular calves.

His head is shaven all around except for a swath that begins at the crown of his head and is woven into a thin braid that swings between his shoulders. He also has a brown mustache that he used to let me twirl the ends of when I was smaller. Babushka says he's a romantic figure, and I thought she meant she was in love with him. I laughed really hard, but she corrected me.

"A romantic figure is someone who is an ideal, like a hero from the past. He represents a time when Cossacks rode the steppes, and fought off the invading hordes. Ivan still has that in him."

I know a little about Cossacks, but this one doesn't ride a wild pony, wield a sword, and wear ballooned pants. This one makes the best fish tacos and vegetarian dishes from a yellow and rusted food truck.

Tato draws me away as the argument goes on.

"Sofiya," he says. "I want to put you fully in charge of bringing this camp to life."

I nod. I know Tato is trying to distract me from the commotion. But it still feels like an honor for him to fully trust me with the idea.

Tato fishes in his pocket and extracts the keys to the dolphinarium. "I'm going to stay here for a little while. But you need to get going. Ilya will be there soon. Don't start anything before I get there. The dolphins are on a strict training schedule and we need to plan this while sticking to their routine. The weekend staff will be there, too. Just stay out of trouble."

"Okay." I can't be angry with him right now. Everyone is so serious and worried.

There's another commotion, and I see Ivan marching up to a group of men, his mustache bristling with anger.

In Ukrainian, he cries to them, "You want to talk to me? Talk to me in Ukrainian!"

The men back off and walk away, throwing words over their shoulders like the last of a handful of pebbles. Ivan puts his hands on his hips, then turns to the crowd and waves a finger at the people milling around the truck.

"Ukrainian, you hear? Our language is our weapon!"

That's what Babushka has said to me on more than a few occasions. Tato, too, when I complained about confusing Russian and Ukrainian grammar.

"We can't forget our language, Sofiya. It is our only defense. Our shield! We fought hard to have a right to it after the Soviet days!"

I never understood it then. I think I'm starting to now.

Just as I cross the street, I see that very same slogan graffitied on the back of a stop sign, like an echo.

Мова—наша зброя! Mova-nasha zbroya! Language is our weapon!

Miss Yvette tells us something similar; that language is power, and opens doors. Babushka and Tato mostly speak Ukrainian to me because since Ukraine became independent, it has been allowed. Before, under the Soviet Union, Ukrainians could not learn or work in their language. They had to function in Russian. And language as a weapon is something I've heard over and over since I was a kid. It makes me think of Colin. It makes me think about Tato's experiments in teaching Roxi real language. I wonder . . . I wonder if that isn't the kind of power—the kind of defense—the dolphins could really use . . .

CHAPTER 11

A New Language

It's another long walk to the dolphinarium. This time, I'm mulling over what Miss Yvette said to us. That the protest at the Maidan had called for our president to quit. But he has fled the country instead. And abandoning an entire country is pretty terrible, just like a mom abandoning her child.

I think of the photos I've seen from the protest in Kyiv. Our capitol is so far away, so I don't feel scared even though I feel like I should. Nothing has really changed, has it? At least Ilya hasn't, because when I arrive, his face is as sour as always.

"You're late!" He snaps his gum.

"Sorry," I mutter. "Did you hear what happened?"

He looks blankly at me for a second, but then he says, "Who hasn't?"

I'm about to say something more about our president, but he tilts his chin up at me. There is this sharp look in his eye, like he's ready for a fight. I remember what Babushka told me last night about him and, instead, I yank the door open.

I head into the lower level of the dolphinarium. Ilya and I are submerged in the lagoon again. Finally, things feel peaceful. All the dolphins and Fizz are together. Ilya is watching them behind the glass as I unpack my bag. I sit on the floor next to a big pillar. I have my observation journal where I've made a to-do list. Now, with Tato's blessing, we have a lot of work to do.

"Listen, we're going to offer a kids' camp over the spring holidays and get a bunch of kids in who will learn how to work with the dolphins."

Ilya scowls. "What? Why?"

"Because their parents will be busy working," I answer impatiently. "Besides, the dolphins like working with kids. And working with dolphins makes *most* people feel good,"

Ilya rolls his eyes.

"What we need to do is make an internet page specifically for this camp, where kids can register." I look up at Ilya.

I pause, remembering what Ivan Markovych said. Language is our weapon. It's our defense. There is a tingling in me, like bells going off but I'm inside them.

Ilya waves a hand in my face. "Hello? And what do you want me to do about it?"

"About . . . ? About what?" I shake myself off.

"The *website*," he sighs.

"Design it." I hold up a printed sheet of his soccer club's website. "You made this for your club, didn't you?"

He frowns but nods. He takes a few steps toward me and squats down.

"It's good," I say. "I think the idea is that you do something similar for this camp. Because we need to raise funds for the dolphinarium and for Colin's birthday show."

"Colin," he mutters, and glances toward the glass.

"The one you played with yesterday."

He scowls. "I didn't play—"

"Next, we should have a live camera on the dolphins so that people can click on it and watch from home. My tato got the idea from a dolphinarium in America. People got more interested in the dolphinarium and started visiting it, mostly because their kids loved watching the dolphins. So we can set up cameras around the pools. We just need to download the app to our phones, so that we can post videos. We need links to those cameras so anyone can watch what we're doing here. How we work, what the dolphins do—"

"Watch them sleep," Ilya mocks.

I ignore him because I'm getting excited. Even though he's still got his arms folded in front of him, I catch another gleam in his eye. A good one this time, like he's interested, even if he's still acting like he doesn't care.

"Then, we need to plan Colin's birthday show."

He stands up. "Colin's birthday show? I can't plan a

dolphin birthday. I don't know anything about training dolphins."

"Well, you would if you knew how to talk to them," I say. I get up and show him the book. It's my observation journal. My tato has one, too.

"I've been doing a lot of research, and here are some of my ideas," I explain.

Ilya peers at the page. "You want to teach the dolphins sign language? Like they're deaf, or what?"

"We are already teaching them. My tato has been practicing with Roxi for a couple of months now. And if kids could see us communicating with dolphins, maybe it would drum up more interest for the camp."

Ilya looks at the lagoon, then at me, his expression full of disbelief.

I grab the computer tablet from my backpack. As I open up the YouTube app, Ilya comes behind me and looks over my shoulder. The video is already queued.

I click on the arrow to play the video, and I start explaining. "There's a research center in Hawaii that's been working with a dolphin, using sign language. They have a TV in the wall of the pool and can even give signals from underwater over a TV monitor."

Ilya makes a shushing sound and I turn the tablet to him so

he can watch the video. I've already seen it a dozen times. We move to one of the benches and sit down, silent as Ilya watches the documentary.

When it's over, Ilya's head is bouncing up and down. He looks at me. "So, how do you plan to do this?"

"I thought we could videotape me—" I stop. "Or us . . . giving sign language commands to Colin. But you would be my guinea pig . . . to see if Colin will take commands from a . . . well, another kid."

His eyebrows knit together.

I go to my backpack and return with the picture cards I borrowed from Tato's home office. "My tato has been recording the hand signals for months now. He wrote about it in his observation journal. It's like what kids use to learn new vocabulary in a new language. But Miss Yvette once said that the building block to language is word order. So why not have Colin and the pod learn entire sentences?"

Ilya is studying the hand signals for *through*, *hoop*, *person*, *surfboard*, and *fetch*.

"Isn't this the same as training them to do tricks?" Ilya asks slowly.

I shake my head. "It's different." And it's like we both know why without having to say it. This wouldn't be as simple as teaching them commands. They would be able to understand us, and we would be able to understand them. Protect them. Who knows what they might have to say?

Ilya blinks first. "Don't dolphins talk to each other underwater? Isn't that how they communicate?"

I nod. "Yeah. But they don't talk. They don't have vocal chords. They use their blowholes to make all their noises."

"They have a lot of different calls, don't they?" Ilya asks.

I'm pleasantly surprised at how much he knows. "As a matter of fact, like cats, dolphins in captivity have a wider range of noises they can make because of their contact with humans and their environment. Which is what got these scientists onto the idea that dolphins develop language similar to humans."

"Or cats."

"Or cats. So why not sign language?"

Ilya slowly goes up to the glass. Colin suddenly appears with the red ring in his beak and nods to Ilya.

Ilya puts a hand on the glass, his palm flat. "Do you think that Colin could actually manage?"

Somehow, it feels like Ilya's asking for himself as well. "If anyone will manage to learn a new language, it's going to be Colin. And you can learn it, too." *If you do what I tell you,* I think.

I step up to the glass. Ilya looks at me, and his mouth twitches into a smile. The green specks in his eyes are bright, like glitter.

"You want to help?" I ask.

"Let's try it," he says.

CHAPTER 12

Swimming with Dolphins

Upstairs, we're just about to get Colin into the experimental pool when Tatyana walks in.

"Does your father know about this?" she asks.

I instinctively lift up the book he lent me. "He agreed that we can try this out with Colin."

She raises her eyebrows, but nods. Tato has a history of letting me do things that other parents might not let their kids do. In this case, I'm just going to assume Tato would let me use his sign language notes.

"We've got to be quick," I whisper to Ilya. "And then I'm going to go swim with the dolphins before my tato gets here."

While Tatyana opens the gate, I pull out the rest of the big cardboard cards with the hand signals. We have to do this as a team, Ilya and I. So we first practice the hand signals together. When we get through the cards, we each pick out two. Colin swims through the gate. The rim of this pool is high, so we can lean in close to Colin. It's the closest I've seen Ilya get to Colin yet. And he hasn't even flinched.

I suddenly realize that both Colin and Ilya have a dark past.

Colin's training as a soldier is something I can only guess at, based on Ilya's reactions to him. But are Ilya's losses what Colin senses? Like Colin senses how much I miss my mom? Is that why Colin tossed the ring to him?

Ilya's voice interrupts my thoughts again. "I've got *hoop* and *through*." He holds up the cards.

I hand him *fetch* and *Frisbee*, then throw the big square hoop and a Frisbee into the water. Colin swims over and noses each of them.

"Communicate with Colin," Ilya says. "It'd be a cool name for the course."

I peer at him and can't help but smile. "Yeah," I agree. "It would."

"So, how are you going to get Colin to listen to me?" he asks.

My heart soars suddenly. I'm really excited. "Up until now, we've used whistles and our hand signals. So he knows what the whistle means and our hand signals for certain movements, but he has to learn the sign language from you. You have to show him the *fetch* signal first. I'll blow, you make the hand signal again. When he comes back with the Frisbee, you'll give him a fish as positive reinforcement."

Ilya looks uncertain but steps up to the rim of the pool. I put the whistle to my mouth.

"Are you ready?"

"Yeah."

"Call his name."

"Colin!"

Colin's head pops up, and he angles it like a dog waiting for a bone. Ilya holds a finger up, like I've taught him, which all the dolphins know means to pay attention and wait for a signal.

"Now!" I call. "Hand signal first."

Ilya makes the signal for *fetch* and Colin chatters. Before Colin gets distracted, I blow the whistle for *fetch* and Ilya repeats the same hand signal. Colin pushes away, swims to the Frisbee, and brings it back to Ilya.

"Now give him the signal for *Frisbee*," I say.

Ilya is smiling nervously. When Colin comes back with it, he reaches for the Frisbee but suddenly jerks his hand back. Finally, Ilya lifts the Frisbee out of the water while proudly making the hand signal.

We repeat this multiple times. *Signal. Whistle. Signal. Whistle.*

Then I put my whistle down and let Ilya signal on his own.

Fetch, Ilya signals.

It works! Colin fetches the Frisbee with Ilya's hand signals without me having to blow the whistle. We do the same thing with *hoop* and *through*. This takes much longer, though, and I can see Ilya is getting frustrated.

"It takes time," I say, tossing Colin a fish before he gets frustrated, too. "Just give it time."

Ilya nods. "What's next?"

"Now let's see whether Colin will fetch the hoop with the hand signals alone."

"Colin!" Ilya calls. He's really smiling now.

Colin pops up. He's waiting, his eye on Ilya and not on me. Ilya says, "Fetch! Hoop!" while making the hand signals.

Colin clicks at him, but he doesn't go. Ilya looks at me, disappointed.

"Try again," I say.

"Fetch! Hoop!" Ilya repeats while he signs.

Again, Colin clicks, his head bobbing in the water. But he doesn't move.

Ilya doesn't look back at me this time. He looks directly at Colin as he raises his hands and signs, *Fetch hoop!*

Colin pushes away and I hold my breath. He ducks down into the water before popping up, grabbing the floating hoop, and swimming it back over to Ilya.

"Yay, Colin!" we both shout. We're jumping up and down as Colin chirps through his blowhole, shoveling water at us.

Ilya laughs. "Your fish is coming, it's coming!"

"Good boy, Colin! That's it!" I reach over and stroke him. Ilya is still smiling. "Good job, Ilya. You did really well. I *really* think this could work!"

"It's pretty cool. But . . . are you actually going to swim with them now?"

I pat Ilya's shoulder as I head for the locker room. "You only have to watch."

Colin is in the show pool with the rest of the pod now. They're all swimming around, excited. They know someone is going to play with them.

Ilya stands far away from the pool in an oversize rubber apron so he doesn't get wet, and I can't help but laugh.

I slide into the water. It's cold but only for a little bit. The pod makes a big circle around me when I'm a few feet away from the rim of the pool, and one after the other, they swim by me for strokes.

Ilya is bug-eyed, watching me. "How . . . how do they feel?"

"Like big hot dogs," I joke.

He frowns, but that smile of his, it's coming.

Colin swims on his back past me, chirping. He makes an *ah-ah-ah* sound and "claps" his fins together.

Ilya laughs now, but his arms are still crossed in front of him. Then Colin submerges. Barking Pesyk is next. Lily comes right behind Roxi. I introduce each of the dolphins to him.

"Lily and Roxi are the babies. They're only two and three years old."

"How can you tell which is which?"

"You just can," I say. I glance up at him, and Ilya's face has gotten dark again. I try again. "Do you see the skin of the young ones? Their skin is super-firm and fresh. If you look at Colin, you can see spots everywhere. Like age spots on older people. And Pesyk, well, you can tell by the white spot on his melon. That's what we call their foreheads."

"What's the scratch on Lily's face?" Ilya asks.

"Her mom bit her."

"What?" Ilya shakes the bangs out of his eyes to take a closer look. "Her mom bit her?"

"Lily swam too far away from her mom, so her mom grabbed her by the face and bit hard. Kind of a way to remind her who's the boss and that she has to stay close. It's a part of her now, and it's how I can quickly tell Roxi and her apart. But you can also tell the difference by their dorsal fins and their flukes—the tails."

Suddenly, I think about some of Colin's scars. Ilya's father's words ring in my ears again. *Colin is a nurse now and not a soldier.* What kind of dangerous situations had he been in as a soldier? The thought makes my stomach hurt.

"Can you tell by their voices, too?" Ilya interrupts my thoughts.

I peer at him. His curiosity is kind of cool, but it also makes me feel protective of the pod. "I told you dolphins don't have vocal chords. All their noises come through their blowholes. But here's something. Did you know that mama dolphins give their babies names? And those names last a lifetime?"

Ilya snorts. "What? For real?"

"For real," I say. "The dolphins introduce themselves to each other like we do. And when a dolphin has a baby, the mama gives a male dolphin a name"—I make air quotes—"that sounds very similar to her own. That way, if he happens to meet her later, he knows that it's his mom, and not a potential female mate."

"Ew!" Ilya groans.

I laugh. "And girls get a name that's very different from the mom."

Colin comes up again and this time, he places his beak against my cheek, like he's giving me a kiss.

Again, Ilya doesn't seem to know how to react. He steps forward, then steps back, furiously chewing a piece of gum.

The dolphins are all chirping and whirring now. It's really loud, so I have to call over the noise and the water. "Pesyk! I want a hug," I say as he swims toward me. He stops, "barks," and presses up against me, his fins on my upper arms.

"Aww, thank you," I say, and give him a peck on his rostrum.

"Don't you have to give them fish?" Ilya asks. He's reaching for the bucket.

"Being kind and complimenting them is sometimes enough," I say. "They'll get fish later, after they've worked. Right now, though, you can give them ice cubes. There's a bucket over there."

Ilya walks back with the metal bucket of ice cubes and I watch as he calls to the dolphins. Colin comes up first, opens his mouth, and Ilya tosses the ice cube. It hits Colin on the beak and goes into the water, but Colin dives after it.

"Try again," I call as Pesyk comes up next. The girls now see what is going on and are heading over, too. Ilya slips Pesyk an ice cube first, then steps closer and gives one to each of the girls. This time he stays at the edge of the pool instead of backing off.

But now it's my time. With my whistle, I signal that I want to swim. The dolphins circle lazily. I pull the goggles down over my eyes and stick the snorkel into my mouth. This is my favorite part.

Underwater, everything slows down. Underwater, there is just nothing—absolutely nothing—that can go wrong.

The dolphins are below me, and I don't care what Ilya is doing above. I let myself sink a little lower. The world above is closed away. It's only the pod and me here now. Everything goes into slow motion. Even the dolphins are swimming more slowly. After a few minutes, Colin twists over onto his back and looks at me with invitation. I nod, pull out my snorkel, and let it float up. He makes another pass.

I latch onto his dorsal fin as we glide through the water.

Dolphins are powerful swimmers, and pretty soon, I feel like I am on an underwater Ski-Doo. But I know what I have to do with my body to make this work, how to make sure it's comfortable for Colin, too. I've been doing it since I was three.

Colin slows down, and I let go, swimming up to him so that we are nearly eye to eye. I wave and go back up for air.

"Wow!" Ilya cries. He's clapping wildly. "That was wild! Amazing!"

I start to laugh, embarrassed by the memory of the very first time I did this. I was wearing a two-piece suit. When I came out of the water, I only had one piece left on me. But I was little. Maybe four or five years old.

"What's so funny?" Ilya asks.

"Nothing." I am not going to tell him this story. The last thing I need is for Ilya to have something he can really embarrass me with. But I can't stop laughing. And this time I laugh because this, being in the pool with my pod, makes me happiest. I can't help it. It's like when you've heard a really, really funny joke and you can't stop laughing.

It takes a while, but finally, the giddiness passes.

"Toss them some more ice cubes," I say to Ilya. Roxi and Lily pick up on the bucket, and this time, Ilya aims carefully and they get the ice right into their beaks.

"Like dogs, you said," he laughs.

"Hey!" I raise my hand into a high five. "You did great today. I think we could really get Colin to understand whole sentences in no time!"

Ilya smacks me a high five back and I'm about to go change when the door to the lagoon opens. Major Chaban strides in like he owns the place.

"Ilya Ilyich, do you know what time it is? I told you to come here and tell them you're not doing the project and then come back home!"

I look at Ilya, open-mouthed.

Tato comes in from the side door and greets Major Chaban. But Ilya's father hardly acknowledges mine.

"Ilya, it's time to go," Major Chaban snaps. "This project isn't going to happen anyway. I'll make sure Director Vovk drops any disciplinary actions on you."

Tato puts his hands on his hips. "Excuse me, but I do believe last time I checked, I am the director of the dolphinarium, and this project and this camp are not going to be canceled."

Major Chaban scowls. "With President Yanukovych gone, Sevastopol will be a part of Russia again. We both know that the dolphinarium is going broke. The Russian Federation will make sure to secure the Black Sea coasts, so I've made recommendations for the navy to take over the dolphinarium. These animals will be assessed for military marine training."

Ilya and I look at each other, and I snap my mouth shut.

"Don't you think you're jumping ahead?" Tato argues. His tone is measured but I can tell he's angry by the way his eyebrows come together over his nose.

"No. I am not jumping ahead. It's long overdue. You'll see who has the majority here. When Sevastopol is a military base again, you'll either comply or move off the peninsula. Ilya, let's go!"

But Ilya is rooted to his spot. Roxi and Lily are chirping and whirring, and Major Chaban strides over. He shoves Ilya toward the door. But Ilya looks at me over his shoulder. We lock eyes.

Either he knew about his father's plans or he is as surprised as I am. I can't tell. All I know is, if our president doesn't come back, my pod is in danger.

CHAPTER 13

The Russians

Tato is sullen in the car on the way home. I am, too. But it's with me—not Major Chaban—he's raising issue with.

"I told you, you were not to do any training without me," he says.

"But we didn't work too long—"

"But, but, but, Sofiya!"

"Tato, listen! Colin can do it! He learned to fetch the Frisbee and I'm sure, if we'd had more time, he'd have been able to go through the hoop, too, with just a little more practice."

"No, Sofiya."

"What do you mean 'no'?"

"I said no. Not without my supervision. If you want to do this, you do it with supervision." He pulls out onto the road, his eyes staring straight ahead, but his brows are like crossed knives over his nose.

"Fine." I pout. "When? When can you supervise? When will there ever be enough time?"

He bangs the steering wheel with the heel of his palm. "Sofiya, I have a lot of other things I need to do right now."

"What about Major Chaban?" I ask, and my voice is

shaking. "What did he mean back there? About taking over the dolphinarium? How would he be able to do that?"

Tato's face turns red and he snaps, "Major Chaban doesn't know what he's talking about. Just ignore him."

But I'm not so certain he's telling the truth.

"Is it about the president?" I ask quietly.

No answer.

Instead of coming in and making dinner, Tato parks the car at our house and tells me to warm up some food with Babushka. "I'm going to be at Ivan Markovych's. Don't wait up."

I hesitate, but he reaches over and pulls me in, his face all soft now. He kisses the top of my head. "Don't worry, Sofiya. And about Colin, I'll make time to work with you and Ilya."

He *is* distracted.

"I need someone else who can help me train the hand signals," I remind him. "Ilya isn't coming back. It was fun doing it with . . . with another kid," I admit.

Tato sighs and looks out the windshield. It's starting to snow. "Why don't you ask your other friends from school?"

I give him a hopeful look. I guess I could ask Cedric, Anna, and Petro. But to my surprise, the thought of Ilya not being my training partner anymore makes me feel sad, like a missed opportunity. Opportunity for what, though? I don't know.

"Sure," I say.

"But when I'm there. Let's say on Thursday." He starts the engine of our car. "Maybe you can teach Colin the signal for *run away from Major Chaban*."

I laugh. But the more I think about it, the more this doesn't seem like such a bad idea.

I feed Neptune and get myself ready for school. But the news on the radio makes me stop before I lock the door. The way they're talking—those radio announcers—makes me wonder whether Tato really has no reason to worry.

When I get to school, Anna, Cedric, and Petro are all waiting for me and pounce on me with questions.

"Did you hear?" Anna calls as I'm locking up my bike.

"We don't have a president," Petro says softly as I walk up.

"He just left the country!" Cedric is leaning against the landing. "He's hiding in Moscow!"

Just like my mother, I think.

"Vladimir Putin is going to come," I say, "and take Crimea from Ukraine."

Cedric and Anna gape at me. Petro frowns. It was one of the last things the man on the radio said. If he does, then Major Chaban may be right. The Russian navy could surely seize Colin and the pod for their purposes. Turn Colin back into a soldier . . .

Then I freeze suddenly.

Across from us, Ilya and his clique from Russian Hill are lounging around the steps. Ilya is watching me, and for a second, it's just me and him. I want to charge over there, ask him how he can let his father even make the suggestion that he would seize our animals. But I don't. He says nothing, no signal, no movement. But two of his friends move away from the landing as a group of students make their way up the stairs. Both boys have wrapped Russian flags around their shoulders—white, blue, red.

"Crimea is Russia," one of them says at a group of kids passing by. Like it's a fact.

The second one pumps his fist in the air and shouts like he's cheering at a soccer game. *"Rossiya! Rossiya!"* Russia! Russia!

Feeling sick, I turn away from the spectacle. Cedric, Anna, and Petro are all watching me. I can't talk about what happened yesterday. I just can't. *Run away!* I think, and shiver. Language—it really could be our best defense.

"Come on," I say. "We'll be late for English."

Miss Yvette meets us at the door and gives us a look as if to say, *I told you so.*

As we take our seats, she stands at the front, and for a while everyone is just quiet. Finally, she sighs and says, "Kids, I don't know what to say, but this could be good or it could be bad. I think it could be good. The people in Kyiv are already talking about replacing the president with someone more pro-Western, pro-Ukrainian."

Petro raises his hand but glances over at me when Miss Yvette calls on him. "Is Sevastopol going to become part of the Russian Federation?"

Miss Yvette gets a funny look on her face. "Let's hope it doesn't come to that, okay?"

"Kyiv is so far away. What if they can't do anything to help us?" Cedric says. "My dad might lose his job."

Anna is defiant and stands up. "Ukraine is a free and independent country, and Crimea is part of it!"

"Only because someone made a mistake," says a boy in the back.

I turn in my chair. It's Vova. He's from Russian Hill, too, like Ilya and his clique. He's usually pretty nice, and quiet, and wears glasses with brown metal frames. But right now, he's staring at Miss Yvette as if to challenge her.

Miss Yvette looks down at her feet before slowly looking back up at us. In English, she says, "I think for today, that's enough speculation."

Then she gets up and writes on the board. *S-P-E-C-U-L-A-T-I-O-N* and beneath, *to guess an outcome without knowing the facts.*

When she turns back to us, she straightens. "Unfortunately, the decisions are not left up to you, yet. They will be some day, when you're old enough to vote. And then when it's your turn, I hope that you all remember who you really are. And how we can try to better understand each other in this world."

She looks at Vova.

"I know who I am. I'm Russian," he mutters.

"And some of your peers are Ukrainian," Miss Yvette stresses. "We're all people."

She looks in my direction where Cedric, Anna, and Petro are clustered around my table.

"You need to learn that and you need to stick together," she finishes.

I don't see Ilya Chaban again, except from a distance. There's no sign from him, no signal, that he knows I, or the dolphins, exist. Like Sunday never happened. But why did he spend nearly half a day with me at the dolphinarium when he knew he was supposed to go home?

That night, Tato and I sit down to dinner and finally have time to talk. He tells me again that everything is going to be okay. I know he's trying to make it seem like everything is normal, but the only thing that keeps my mind from worrying is when we start to talk about the camp and sign language training. As if somehow, if I can figure out a way to communicate with Colin, anything is possible. That the Russian navy ships in the water might sail away and the men from Russian Hill might go to Ivan's truck just to buy his tacos.

He talks to me about how he's worked with Roxi. Though I've seen him do it, I never really concentrated on all the steps.

"If you do this properly, Colin could learn very quickly," he tells me. "But your friends must learn all the hand signals correctly. They'll be our test group to see if Colin can understand the signals from people he doesn't know as well."

I nod. "We'll practice."

"Under my supervision," he says, eyebrows raised.

That night, Tato goes out again. I don't know where he is but I'm not worried, because there's a note telling me not to worry, so I know that he'll be home at some point.

On Tuesday, I convince my friends to help me with the training. I decide not to tell them about Ilya, or about Major Chaban, or how Major Chaban pulled Ilya out of the project and threatened my tato and me. They're already excited and get permission to go to the dolphinarium with me.

On Thursday, after fifth period, the four of us cut through the park to the main road. But when we reach the traffic circle, a long line of trucks snake their way around and toward the city center. It's a convoy of green military vehicles. The people on the pavement turn and watch. They start murmuring to one another. Two men hold up their cell phones and start making videos.

"They're headed for the naval base," a woman says to the gathering crowd.

Anna and Petro gape and lock eyes with each other. "Tato!" they say at the same time.

Their dad, a Ukrainian navy captain, is on that base.

A group of men dressed in regular clothes march around the corner across the street holding white, blue, and red flags stretched out between their hands. The two men who were making videos of the vehicles step aside and turn to each other.

"Let's go get our guys," one of them says. They take off and run across the park. We kids look at one another. We all know there is going to be a fight.

"We should go to the naval base," Anna whispers to Petro. "Check on Tato."

But my mind goes immediately to Major Chaban's threats. The light turns green and I dash across the street.

"I have to get to the dolphinarium! I have to save the dolphins!"

As I run ahead, the others start calling out questions to me, wanting to know what I mean. But I'm already sprinting.

We get to the dolphinarium and that's when I slow down. There are no military trucks. Nothing but the usual quiet parking lot awaits us. The staff entry is locked so I use the spare key Tato gave me on Sunday. I throw the door open and wave Cedric, Anna, and Petro inside.

But Petro is on his cell phone, tapping out a message. Anna is looking over his shoulder. It's probably to their dad.

"Come on," I say. I'm feeling frantic.

Cedric follows me, but Petro and Anna are lagging behind us.

"What is going on, Sofiya? Save the dolphins from what?" Cedric asks.

"From the Russian military," I cry. "Ilya's father said that if the Russians take over Crimea, they'll take the dolphins back."

"Take them back where? For what?" Anna asks. She pushes her dark bangs out of her face as she comes abreast.

"They'll retrain them for the military, to be spies!"

Petro sticks his phone into his jeans pocket.

"Colin was a soldier," I tell them. "He was a Soviet-trained spy before he was turned into a therapy dolphin."

Anna and Cedric just gape at me, but Petro walks up to the glass. Pesyk swims by.

"Were they military marine mammals?" Petro asks me.

"You know about them?" I ask.

"Yeah, sure. I read about them a while ago. Remember,

Anna? Tato told us about the MMS program? The Ukrainian navy has a couple at the base. They patrol their harbor."

Anna's eyes go wide. "That's right. I forgot." She looks at Petro again at the mention of their tato. What if those military vehicles really were going straight for the navy base where he works?

Petro's phone pings right then, and he whips it out. He looks over at Anna. "He's okay. He says not to worry."

I'm starting to believe that's what all adults say to us kids.

Now Cedric is looking through the glass. The dolphins have noticed us and are all taking passes.

"A spy . . ." he murmurs. "We're swimming with spies."

The door opens and Tato appears. "What's going on here?"

"What if the Russians really come and seize the dolphins?" I ask after we tell him about the convoy.

My tato scratches his beard. "Sofiya, will you trust me? We'll never let somebody just seize our pod. Not the dolphins. Not Fizz. Not the sea lions. Come now. You guys are kids. You shouldn't be worrying about this." He puts a super-friendly smile on for my friends. "Now . . . let's say we go and train Colin in sign language?"

His words seem to give us all some relief. Even me, for now.

I show Cedric, Anna, and Petro what Ilya and I had started to do with Colin. But I don't tell any of them about Ilya having been here. I just don't want them to know. And Tato doesn't say anything either. By the time I get changed, he's already taught my friends some of the main hand signals.

Tato brings Roxi into the experimental pool first and shows us how it's done. He signs for Roxi to swim through the hoop. Then he tells me to get into the water.

"Now watch this," Tato says. "I'm going to tell Roxi to pick up Sofiya, then take her to the surfboard over there."

My friends laugh excitedly, but I swim out a little way, concentrating. Tato has a blindfold over his eyes so that Roxi can't read his facial expressions—which is what the dolphins really focus on. That or whistles. Now she has to pay attention to his hands.

"Roxi," he says, holding his finger in the air for her to wait. *Fetch, person, surfboard,* he signs.

Roxi dives down and swims underneath me. I feel a rush of excitement as she scoops me up and I ride in front of her dorsal fin to the surfboard. She swims back, to the applause of the kids, and gets her treat and congratulations.

Tato turns to Cedric, Anna, and Petro. They're all beaming.

"Now watch this. We'll reverse it. Roxi!" *Fetch, surfboard, person.*

This time Roxi brings the surfboard to me.

I swim back after a few more of these. The kids are clamoring around my tato.

"Why aren't all the dolphins being trained like this?" Cedric asks him.

"They will be. It's something we began experimenting with," Tato says. "So we test it out on one dolphin before we decide whether or not to apply that learning to the other dolphins. We really want them to learn language. To fully understand us. So, Roxi was simply up to the task when I took it on. But I think Sofiya is right. She and Colin have a special bond. If he's going to learn from anyone, it's going to be her. Especially with your help."

"And if we film the process with the cameras you bought, Tato," I suggest, "it could be a great way to advertise the camp and raise money for the dolphinarium." *Enough money to keep Major Chaban as far away as possible*, I think to myself.

Tato nods. "One thing at a time."

Now it's Colin's turn. He swims right up to me when I call, clicking and whirring. I know I'm supposed to cover my eyes before training, but I can't help it. When Colin and I lock eyes, he looks at peace. But I'm pleading with him, *Please, please, please*, in my head. He suddenly pushes away from the rim and rises up. He is quiet, like he's waiting. Like he's really listening. I know that he is going to do what I need him to do. I even think he knows the urgency involved.

I pull my blindfold down over my eyes, and trust him. *Fetch Frisbee!* I sign.

Anna laughs next to me, and I yank off the blindfold to see that Colin is returning with the Frisbee.

She throws an arm over my shoulder. "Who knows, maybe we'll teach him adjectives and adverbs, too. *Fetch the green Frisbee quickly. Fetch the red frisbee slowly.*"

Everyone loves the idea, especially Tato. And the basics keep working! Colin makes only a couple of mistakes in the next round of commands with Anna.

"It's okay, Colin," I whisper to him as he bobs in the water. "Everyone makes mistakes. You're doing so great."

We do another round and this time, even though I'm blindfolded, I know he's in tune with me. I can visualize him. And Colin doesn't make a single mistake.

Tato has that super-pleased look on his face. "This is really amazing, Sofiya. Amazing."

Cedric taps my shoulder. "I'm going to be in so much trouble when I get home."

I look at the clock. I hadn't even realized how late it is.

"I think we can call it a day," Tato says.

We let Colin out into the lagoon with the rest of the pod, Fizz, and the sea lions, and head downstairs. But Colin doesn't want to stop. He swims up to the glass.

"I'm gonna do a trick for Colin for a change," Anna says. She does a cartwheel on the floor in front of the aquarium. She's all legs and arms and dark hair, which she's arranged into two braids today.

All of a sudden, I see Colin suspend himself upside down in the water.

"Ha! Look, Colin is trying to do a cartwheel," Cedric laughs.

Anna straightens and looks at the glass.

"Try it again," Petro says.

"Wait," Cedric calls, and he pulls out his phone. "I'm going to take a video."

Anna does a second cartwheel while Colin follows her. This time, Colin does a *full* circle. Anna laughs and does a third cartwheel. Colin does the same.

Petro gives Colin a wave, and Colin waves back with his flipper. But this is an old trick that we all know.

"Hey, look at this video." Cedric lowers his phone and presses the screen.

"This is really cool," Anna says, looking over his shoulder. "And look." She pulls Petro over and makes him give her his phone. "Petro has a bunch of videos of Colin when he was putting that first full sentence together. Plus, the ones on cameras that your tato bought."

"We could do a series like this," I say. "And put these up, one day at a time, all the way into April and then leading up to camp registration."

"Yeah," Cedric says. "A whole series of vlogs teaching kids how we taught Colin sign language. I can even build a website for you."

I look from one to the other.

"This is a really great idea," Anna calls.

"A really great idea," Petro repeats.

I should be full of excitement. But I can't help thinking of Ilya and how this would mean he is completely out. I'm surprised how sad that makes me.

CHAPTER 14

Little Green Men

It's been weeks since our president ran away and more and more people are talking in whispers. There is graffiti on the walls and buildings. Even the park benches are layered with slogans and bad words. Blue-and-yellow flags are crossed out with red paint and letters spelling *Crimea is Russia!* Those letters are crossed out and a big blue-and-yellow *Ї* is written on top.

"Why the letter *yee*?" I ask Babushka.

"Because it is a Ukrainian letter; it doesn't exist in the Russian alphabet."

I wasn't supposed to hear about it, but Tato and Babushka were talking about clashes on the streets. Peaceful protesters with Ukrainian flags went to the parliament building, and a swarm of "pro-Russian" protesters got into a fight with them. Two people were killed. Others were arrested. Not Russians, though.

Our street, thank goodness, is quiet. It's all happening in the city center. There are pictures in the papers and on TV, with shows and channels that have nothing to do with Kyiv or Ukraine any longer. Now all we get are talk shows from Russia with a lot of older people standing around and shouting. It's like listening to the homeless men in the park when they've drunk too much vodka.

Which is why, when Babushka says we're going to take the bus downtown to shop for an Easter dress, I'm kind of excited to see what everyone's been whispering about.

Near the parliament building, crowds have gathered on the streets. The mood is . . . well, *scary*. A lot of men in green military uniforms are patrolling the corners and buildings with large guns in their hands. There are barricades with big white-and-red stop signs. Babushka mutters something about there not being any badges on their uniforms.

"But they have to be the Russian army," she determines.

"How do you know?" I whisper. Like everywhere, everyone on the bus is whispering.

"Because the Russian army overtook our Ukrainian army a week ago," she says.

I turn to Babushka. "What does it mean, they 'overtook'? How does something like that happen? Like how Mr. Vovk took over as school director?"

"Nothing nearly so peaceful," Babushka says. She's not really paying attention to me.

I look out the window again, at those guns the men in green are carrying. I remember the convoy of military trucks my friends and I saw on the way to the dolphinarium. Nothing has happened to us or the dolphin pod, so I somehow believe Tato. I should just ignore Major Chaban. *All bark and no bite.* That's how Ivan Markovych described his dogs once, but I'm not so sure about these men. These men look like they will bite.

The bus stops as the crowd outside grows, like bread rising. People are swarming down the street and into the square, waving Russian flags. The adults around me are speaking in low voices.

I crane my neck to get a better view. On the outskirts of the barricades in the square, there are smaller groups of people holding Ukrainian flags. I don't know why, but they remind me very much of our little group of outcasts at school. I feel sorry for them. They're outnumbered, but maybe they are smarter and can outwit these very angry people.

"See that bus over there?" a woman sitting behind us asks her neighbor. I turn to see where she is pointing. "It's from Russia. They brought Russians over on a ferry from Krasnodar and then by bus here. They've been planted. They've taken over the entire peninsula, just like in summer."

I look outside. For a moment, I imagine that Mama could be one of those passengers. That she came home to make sure I'm okay.

Another passenger responds. "The bridge to Ukraine's

mainland is closed off. These little green men aren't allowing anyone from mainland Ukraine in."

I peer at the men with the weapons. I don't find them all that little. A man in sunglasses and a military beret is on a podium in front of city hall, but I can't understand what he's shouting into the microphone.

Babushka hisses angrily, "What do these people want from us?"

Then she does something I've never seen her do. She spits on the ground, right on the floor of the bus, and makes the sign of the cross.

I might be half Russian and half Ukrainian, but right now, I feel more protective about the Ukrainian part of me. I'm on the side of the underdogs. Which is completely the opposite of Ilya. Like me, he's nearly half-and-half but lately, in school, he's started behaving like his friends. His gang has been acting doubly superior, like they've personally occupied Sevastopol themselves. It really riles me up.

Babushka tells the bus driver to open the door. He does. We are on the fringes of the square when we get off. I stay really close to her, my hand in hers.

The department store she wants to take me to is on the other side of the long street, so we walk along the less crowded side, in the opposite direction of those marching toward the parliament building. She suddenly stops a woman that she apparently recognizes. To me, she's a stranger.

"Svetlana, what is happening here?" Babushka asks.

The woman has big blond-white hair beneath a black fur cap. She makes a long face. "The Russians call this holding a referendum."

"What do you mean they *call* it a referendum?" Babushka asks.

"What's a referendum?" I ask.

"It's when the people vote on one topic that's not part of the normal election," says a boy's voice.

I know that voice. I spin around. Ilya!

His hands are stuffed into his jeans pockets. Two of his friends are with him, waiting for cues from him. But he gives them none. The three of them may as well be a live Russian flag. Ilya is in his blue coat, the second boy is in a red coat, and the third one, instead of white, though, is wearing silver.

"And what is this vote for?" I ask suspiciously.

"Simple," Ilya says. "Is Crimea Russia? Yes or no. It's a no-brainer. Of course it is. The Russians here can't help it if some stupid Soviet leader decided to give the peninsula to Ukraine, just because Kyiv claimed independence. That was a big mistake on his part."

The other two boys nod and high-five each other, congratulating each other as if they've just proven who's the boss.

"Claimed independence? Claimed?" I challenge. "Miss Yvette taught all of us, including you, Ilya and the Idiots, that Crimea voted to be a part of Ukraine! And Ukraine did not *claim* independence. We fought for it and won, fair and square!"

Ilya's chest expands, his hands are clenched. The other two boys are glaring at me, then at him.

"She called us Ilya and the Idiots," the one in the red jacket complains.

"I heard her," Ilya mutters, and flips his hair back from his eyes.

"Sofiya?" It's Babushka. She is still listening to this Svetlana woman, but she has her eyes on the three boys. She suddenly takes a big step toward them. They can't ignore her. Babushka just has that kind of presence.

"Tell me something." Her eyes are on fire. "Do you give someone a gift and then take it away when you want to play with it?"

Ilya stands his ground, but he is shrinking before my very eyes, chewing gum really fast.

Babushka shakes a finger at the boys. "It is an easy thing to simply parrot what you hear, and repeat what you think you know without having to think! It's a waste of perfectly good brain cells, I tell you."

She snatches the sleeve of my coat and marches me right through the three of them. Up on that stage, the man has been replaced by a woman. She is young-looking, with dark hair pulled back, and a tan coat with sheep wool trim. She shouts into the microphone, punching the air with a fist.

The crowd starts chanting, "*Crimea is Russia!*" The outcasts on the sidelines raise their Ukrainian flags higher. Someone tugs me back, and I cry out.

It's Ilya.

Babushka snatches me back and looks at him sternly. "What do you have to say now?"

"Excuse me, Dr. Len." His eyes are on the ground. "Can I speak to Sofiya for a minute?"

Ilya's two friends aren't paying attention to what's happening. They've melted against the wall of a nearby tea shop. Babushka tilts her head, crosses her arms in front of herself, and narrows her eyes at Ilya. She's surprised. So am I. I've also never seen Ilya Ilyich Chaban be so . . . respectful! He's even keeping his gum quiet.

"It's okay," I say to her. "I'll meet you at the store."

She nods and walks away. I'm left standing alone with Ilya.

CHAPTER 15

Provocateurs

I look back at Ilya when Babushka is gone. Recently, I've had vague memories of him from when we were really young. A boy with light brown hair. It had to be him. I wonder whether Ilya remembers us being friends. Whether he remembers my mother. But I'm not going to be the one to bring it up.

"How are the dolphins? And Colin?" Ilya asks. His neck is bright pink. "Did you keep teaching him new words?"

"Yeah," I huff. What does he think? After a month, and with only a couple of weeks before our planned camp, did Ilya really think I'd stop working on Colin's program just because his dad thinks he's the governor of Crimea? "My tato has been helping. Colin understands full sentences now. If Cedric signals *fetch*—"

"Cedric?" Ilya says my best friend's name like it tastes bad.

"And Anna. And Petro."

"The twins. Then . . ." He scowls at the ground and scuffs his shoe.

He better not be making fun of my friends. His own friends are no longer at the tea shop. They've moved farther down the street with the crowd. But instead of Ilya looking annoyed that they left without him, he looks relieved.

Ilya looks back at me. "What about the cameras?"

"They're already set up," I say.

He nods. "Yeah, I know."

"How do you know?"

"I saw your videos on Telegram. But you only have a hundred followers."

"Petro just set up an Instagram account last week," I argue. "And we already have *over* one hundred followers."

Ilya licks his lips. "Yeah, I didn't think the angles were so good, though. Or the videos. I could maybe . . . I mean, if you still want my help."

"I thought your father didn't want you at the dolphinarium," I say.

Ilya slowly takes off his backpack and unzips it. "Yeah. No. He doesn't. I just . . . I took some of your videos and . . ." He hands me a couple of printed pages. There are balloons and fish, and dolphins in a sea spray, and the big sign that Colin is turning thirty. *Communicate with Colin: Learn to Talk with Dolphins. For real!*

My observation journal is full of notes, and my sketch pad is full of drawings that I worked on with Cedric, but Ilya's designs surprise me. I just don't know how to tell him that Cedric has already started building the website and it's supposed to be ready next week.

"You *can* draw," I say instead. "Why did you make me do your homework? These are really good."

He shrugs. "I wasn't interested in biology. But this . . . I don't know. My teachers say I'm able, I just don't do what I'm supposed to do. Besides, I like cartoons."

Ilya then takes out his cell phone. "But what I really like doing are videos. This is one I edited for my soccer club."

His Telegram account has over one thousand followers! I watch the video, and it's really good. The music is great. And there are over two thousand likes. I look up at him, surprised. And a little jealous.

He's shifting from foot to foot. I suddenly think of the story of his mother's accident, and that when Ilya finally came close to the pool, his fear of the dolphins seemed to have ebbed. Maybe it's because our mothers were friends, or because of the way Ilya seemed to change for the better around the dolphinarium, but it's almost like he *belongs* on this project. I remember how even *Colin* tried to connect with him from the start. Sure, I am a bit jealous but now I believe Ilya should be involved. Maybe there's a talent Ilya has that we could use.

"I like this one," I say, pointing to one where the dolphins are balancing cartoon balloons on their noses. "You could make each one a topic and link each balloon to more information."

His eyebrows go up and he cracks a smile. "Yeah, that would be good."

"And videos," I say, thinking of Cedric's. "We need to vlog more about our progress. We have lots of pictures, too."

Ilya clears his throat. "Then you already have a website for the camp."

"We're working on one. It should go up in a couple of days."

His expression crumbles.

"But there's no reason why you can't work with us," I urge. "I mean, we could use you."

The specks in his eyes are alight. "Really?"

"Yeah. We're meeting on Sunday again. But . . . Ilya, what about your . . . father?"

"I can . . ." He looks around and leans closer. "I can convince him."

"For real?" I ask. Somehow I can't picture Major Chaban being convinced of anything we kids want to do.

"I'll try. Besides, he never said I couldn't go to the dolphinarium. He just said my punishment would be . . . whatever. Just dropped. You want a piece of gum?"

I nod, and he gives me a piece of his Dirol, again

bubblegum flavored. Babushka hates it when I chew gum, but I can just hide it under my tongue or in my cheek until I get home.

I pop it into my mouth and stretch out my hand. He's really close to me. "All right. But we keep our lips sealed on this for now."

"All right."

We shake on it. Both of us have our secrets now, but I know that it's the right thing to do, to have Ilya involved, with or without Major Chaban's approval. I just know it. Besides, we're not breaking the rules, we're just bending them.

After Ilya takes off to find his friends, I head off to meet Babushka at the store. But Babushka isn't at the store she said she would be. I stand outside, waiting for her, looking over that sea of faces and waving flags. Two men wearing camouflage jackets and pants have created a barricade. A handwritten sign says *Security*. A couple of Western journalists are talking to them, a man and a woman. They're speaking English and one has the same accent as Miss Yvette, so I'm pretty sure they're Americans.

"So," the male journalist says to the men in camouflage, "you call yourselves a self-defense unit. What are you protecting Sevastopol from?"

A translator repeats his question in Russian.

"We need these checkpoints to keep out the provocateurs," one of the camouflaged men replies.

The translator repeats in English.

I am pleased that I already understood the American journalist. *Provocateurs* was a word Miss Yvette taught us last week. People who *provoke* conflict, like when you poke a sleeping dragon with a big, fat stick and keep doing it until he gets angry and fights back.

"And who are the provocateurs?" the woman journalist asks.

"People who are coming from Kyiv to cause problems," says the camouflaged man again. His arms are crossed over and resting on his belly. "Like they did at the Maidan. We won't let that happen."

The cameraman suddenly begins panning the street and I see him catch me in his lens.

"So what are you doing with these people?" the male journalist asks the second man in green camouflage.

"We have a special department here."

"You're arresting them?"

"I can't tell you what we are doing with them. It's top secret."

Then the male journalist turns to me and his eyes kind of light up. All of a sudden, there is a microphone beneath my face.

"What about you? Do you believe Crimea is Russia or Ukraine?"

I stare at the microphone. My heart beats in my throat. It's Ukraine of course. But those men in the green uniforms, with their big guns, and their blockades, stare down at me. A "special department." Provocateurs are taken to a "special department."

"I don't know," I say quietly.

The journalist looks disappointed, but I feel much more disappointed with myself. I have to say something, don't I? I'm the smart one.

"I think it will be decided in the vote today," I reply. That's what Babushka said.

"You mean the referendum?" one of the Americans asks.

"Yes. It's a democracy."

"And who do you think will win? Russia or Ukraine?" He has that kind of smile that's not real. And he's lost interest in me.

I look around at the crowd and suddenly my stomach sinks. "Well, if you look at how many people are holding Russian flags and how many are holding Ukrainian flags, it doesn't look good for the Ukrainians."

A loud cheer goes up from the crowd. The cameraman suddenly swings away. People are pointing to the roof of the parliament building. A Russian flag is waving at the top. Earlier, there'd been a Ukrainian flag there.

The two camouflaged men fold their hands in front of them

and I see them look at each other. Their bellies roll like they're laughing behind those masks. It's not a nice laugh. It's a kind of a *ha-ha, I got you!* laugh.

Babushka throws up her hands when she finds me. Turns out she's been searching for me, too. I had been looking for her in the wrong store. But she's bought a dress. It's a *vyshyvanka*—a blue embroidery on a bright yellow fabric. I look at it, then at her.

"Yellow isn't my color," I say.

"Blue and yellow are now your colors. Both of them. This isn't about being pretty. It's about what's right."

At home, I go to my room and toss the plastic bag with the dress on my bed. The world doesn't make sense. Green men. White-blue-and-red flags clashing with the sky blue–and–golden yellow ones of Ukraine. Guns. Provocateurs. Jail. Blood on the streets. The only way I can figure this out is by making a list in my observation journal. On one side, I write down: *I am Ukrainian.* On the other side, I write down: *I am Russian.* And I write. *The Russians are angry, they are mean, they are bullies. They are everything I have been told I should not be. But today, Ilya wasn't mean. He wasn't a bully.*

The Ukrainian side of my list wins. But that doesn't feel like the answer either.

I rip out the paper, tear it up, and throw myself on my bed to draw. It starts to feel better. What I can't put into words, I'm putting into pictures.

I draw the green men, but without any patches on their uniforms. They're not Ukrainian. Not Russian. Just aliens in my world now, determined to create chaos.

CHAPTER 16

97%

A siege is when the enemy surrounds its opponent and doesn't allow them to leave. No supplies come in. No food, no water, no family. The little green men take the parliament. Then the airport. They surround the Ukrainian navy and block them off.

Petro and Anna's father is on the navy base. This time, he *is* in trouble.

On the news, a video shows the little green men loading up weapons and equipment into trucks. Everyone knows they are Russian soldiers, even if they wear no patches and flags on their uniforms. But then the Russian ambassador holds a press conference with Euronews and the European Union. He tells a bald-faced lie on the world news report:

"These are not Russian troops. These are self-defense units. The Russian Federation has nothing to do with this."

President Putin echoes the ambassador's words, and I turn to Tato and Babushka.

"He's lying. I know he is lying. I was there!"

"Of course they are lying," Babushka says. "Everyone knows

they are lying. Even that mayor knows he is lying. The whole world knows it!"

"Then why don't we do something about it?" I ask.

Babushka and Tato look at each other. Tato rubs his face with his hands. Babushka puts an arm around my shoulders. Neither of them say I am wrong.

"We are a democracy at gunpoint," Tato says.

"Oh, the irony!" Babushka laughs, but there is no joy in the sound.

I once learned the word *irony.* To say something in a way that actually means the opposite. Tato explained that it has nothing to do with metal, except "irony does pierce the gut of truth."

So, when Tato tells me, "Ninety-seven percent of the voters chose to become part of Russia," the irony is that citizens here were given the chance to vote, but their choice wasn't one of the options. The voting card didn't include a vote for Crimea remaining part of Ukraine. On top of that, the irony is that Russians, who don't even hold a Ukrainian passport, were able to take part in the vote.

Irony is when a little green man says you have to go vote, and then that little green man holds a gun to your head so that you choose the answer he wants you to choose. Which means you really don't have a choice.

"But this means Major Chaban will take over the dolphinarium!" I cry.

Tato pulls his hands away from his face and stares at me. "I'm not going to let that happen, Sofiya. I won't. He's not even an active military commander. He just goes around having everyone call him "Major." But he'd have to be reactivated first. Besides, the international community will certainly have something to say against this. The United States! The United Kingdom! Europe! Nobody will let Russia just walk onto our peninsula and grab our land! Not with a sham referendum!"

But Babushka looks at him, then at the television, then back at him, and her arm slips away from my shoulder as a big, black cloud passes over her face.

I stop at the Monument to the Sunken Ships on the way to school. There is a large naval ship leaving the harbor. Our Ukrainian flag on the monument has been replaced by a Russian one. I bite my tongue to keep from crying.

When I get to school, I spot Ilya and his clique right away. He turns just as I want to head inside.

"Sofiya!"

But I'm not going to talk to him. I'm too upset about the referendum, about the little green men, about the fact that Crimea now belongs to Russia. Major Chaban predicted this would happen, and the Russians might be lying about the results, but I have a bad feeling that Major Chaban was not lying about seizing the dolphinarium.

I go straight to class and don't look for my friends.

Miss Yvette doesn't greet us kids as she usually does. There are no words on the board. There are no games and activities on the tables. Everything is blank, including her face. I take my seat. Cedric, Anna, and Petro come in a few minutes later.

Cedric sits down next to me. "Where were you?"

"Here," I say.

Petro and Anna take their seats in front of us but turn around and frown at me.

"What's going on?" Anna asks.

I shrug and the room gets all quiet. Everyone is waiting for Miss Yvette to say something.

"How is this result even possible?" Miss Yvette asks in English. She then spins to the board and writes over her head and down to the bottom of the board a huge *9*, then a *7*, and then the *%* sign. *97%*. She looks small in front of it.

Nobody answers. That was the result of the referendum. Ninety-seven percent of Crimeans supposedly voted to become part of Russia.

Cedric raises his hand, but checks around him. Miss

Yvette ignores him. She's staring over the back of our heads. He's the only one with his hand up, and he slowly lowers it when she still does not call on him.

"That," she finally says quietly, "is what is called a rhetorical question. A question we ask to make a point, not because we necessarily get an answer."

She then walks between the rows of desks and on each one, she puts down a crossword puzzle. It's handmade. In the center is a column marked in dark, fat ink. It's the kind of crossword puzzle that reveals a secret word. The words that go across are part of our vocabulary training. There are thirteen words to solve and an = sign between the fifth and sixth rows.

I am about to move over to Cedric, Petro, and Anna to work with them, but suddenly Miss Yvette calls our attention up to the front.

"Sofiya, I want you to work with Vova. Cedric, with Markian. Anna, you're with Sergey. Petro, you're with Antonin." And she continues until we are all mixed up in the class. One clique after another falling apart into groups of threes.

I slowly go to the table where she assigned Vova—the pro-Russian student—and another student named Larissa, who I don't really know. Her clique is always taking selfies and playing with the effects on Snapchat.

"Okay," I say, just like I would with my group. "Let's get to work. Vova, the first row is a long word. A special election for a political topic."

Vova bites his bottom lip, still looking down at the paper, but I can tell he's not seeing what's on it.

"I think we should start with the easy words first," Larissa says.

"Why?" I look at her and wonder if she's looked up from her phone long enough to even pay attention to what's happening in her own backyard.

"Fine." Larissa shrugs. "The first word is *referendum*."

I roll my eyes at her. I asked Vova, not her, but I count out the squares.

"Correct," I say.

We all begin writing a letter into each square. The second *r* in *referendum* is in the first fat square. We keep working. This time, Larissa says nothing when I ask Vova whether he can solve the next word.

We are finished within fifteen minutes. In the squares, our solution is clear.

We all turn away from our table and face the front of the room. Miss Yvette is at the blackboard and writes what we already have on our sheets.

RAZOM = TOGETHER

Then she looks at us and says, "The question is, can you

work together? Can at least ninety-seven percent of you in *this* class work together? At *least*?"

I turn back in my chair and look at my new group. I glance over at Cedric's group, at Anna's, at Petro's. I turn back to Miss Yvette and raise my hand.

"Is that a rhetorical question?" I ask.

"No, Sofiya. Were you, Vova, and Larissa able to work together or not?"

Larissa shrugs. Vova nods. So do a whole lot of other kids. Nobody is shaking their head to say *No*.

"Will you work with them in the next period? Or in our next class?" Miss Yvette asks me. "Or will you go back to your friends? To Cedric, Anna, and Petro?"

I answer truthfully. "I'll want to be with my friends."

"That's right," she says. Her voice is sharp. "Because that is where we are comfortable. But what if you and your friends needed help? What if you couldn't do the assignment alone, but you knew that Vova or Larissa could help? Would you ask them for help then?"

"Why wouldn't I ask you? Isn't that what you're here for?" I ask, even though I understand what she's getting at.

Miss Yvette puts her hands behind her back and lowers her head, like she's thinking. Then she gazes at all of us. We're waiting. We're waiting for the answer.

"What am I here for? I think a lot of people are asking that question in this country right now. What are our leaders here for? What are our teachers here for?"

She points at the blackboard over her shoulder with her piece of chalk. "How many of you in this class want to be Russian now? Because if this number is right, then out of this group of twenty-seven, that would be twenty-six of you."

Nobody moves. Nobody answers. My hand twitches. I think of the journalists who asked me if I thought that Crimea was Russia or Ukraine. Of the little green men with their guns staring down on me. The fear rose out of my gut. I froze then, and I freeze now.

"Go on. Raise your hands. Who wants to now hold a Russian passport and be a part of the Russian Federation instead of a citizen of Ukraine?"

There is a very uncomfortable moment in the room, but Vova slowly raises his hand. Then Antonin does.

Miss Yvette smiles tightly at them. "Good. Thank you. Now, can you tell us why?"

"In English?" Vova asks.

"Of course, in English. This is English class."

"Because my parents are Russian, and they want to be in Russia. Crimea is really nice, and they want to stay here."

We titter. Miss Yvette quiets us.

"And you, Antonin?" she asks.

"Same as Vova. My parents want to be Russian citizens in Russia."

"Anyone else's parents here have said they want to be Russians now?"

Nobody else raises their hand.

"Come on," Miss Yvette calls. "At least twenty-six of you in this class do. According to our officials."

I squirm and sit on my hands now. No way. Not me. Not if it means Major Chaban tells the Russian navy to take my dolphins. And I feel a pang, realizing I'm practically betraying my mother. I drop my head. I wonder what she is thinking of all this right now. Does she even care what happens to us?

Miss Yvette sets the chalk on her desk and walks to the front of it, then leans against it. "Do you know what I learned at the Maidan?"

The whole class kind of sighs with relief. We know her stories from the Maidan. Now, this is the Miss Yvette we know.

"*I* learned," she starts, "that if you want to change something, then you need to stay and help *make* that change. Loud enough that your leaders hear you. You make sure changes happen. Because anything worth fighting for must be fought for together. Sometimes the people who fight alongside you will be people you thought were fighting against you. But if you take the time to get to know them . . ." She shrugs. "Who knows?"

Cedric's hand shoots up into the air and he waves it. "Me!"

Miss Yvette looks at him and shakes her head. "No, Cedric. *That* was a rhetorical question again."

At lunch, the Russian Hill brats are playing with a soccer ball. I look up from where I'm squatting on the ground, sifting tiny pebbles into a crack in the asphalt. Ilya kicks the ball high. It flies in our direction, but one of the other boys catches it quickly. I know that I told Ilya he could come back and help out at the dolphinarium, but so much has happened since then. In biology, we had to sit through a boring slide show of historic Russian scientists while the Russian Hill brats gloated. Every slide had the Russian flag in the background. Even though Ilya wasn't one of them, I can't stand the sight of him with them now. I shift positions so that my back is to them and before Ilya can notice me.

"Apparently, Antonin is a Minecraft fan," Petro says. "He's pretty cool."

"Vika is actually kinda cool, too," Cedric says about the girl who was in his group. "Her brother is an MD in Africa now as part of a Doctors Without Borders team."

"I'm going to be a marine biologist," I say, and stand up. "A *Ukrainian* marine biologist."

"Yeah," Anna says softly. "I know."

"We're all Ukrainians," Petro says.

Cedric stuffs his hands into his pockets. "Ummm . . . I'm Nigerian."

"Yeah, but you live in Ukraine," Petro counters.

"Apparently, I now live in Russia."

"That's right. Cedric's got it," someone says. It's Ilya.

I shove past Petro and Anna to get to him. "What do you want?"

Ilya looks surprised. He takes two steps back.

"Did you just come over here to rub something in our faces? That makes you the big guy, right? I'm surprised you're not wearing one of those green coats."

Ilya points at Cedric. "I was just stating a fact, Sofiya. Cedric's father may decide not to teach for a Russian university now that Sevastopol is part of Russia."

I whirl to my best friend. Ilya is right. What if Cedric's family decides they have to move away?

"And what about *our* father," Anna says. "He doesn't even have a choice. He's on the Ukrainian naval base."

"That's right," Petro says. "We haven't seen him in weeks, because the Russians won't let them go."

"I don't have anything to do with that," Ilya says. "I just came over to—"

"Your father is a Russian military officer!" I cry.

"Your *mother* was Russian," Ilya shouts. "And mine was half Ukrainian. So? Now what?"

I clamp my mouth shut. How dare he bring up our mothers?

Petro and Anna actually look like twins now, their arms folded over their chests, their faces masked by the same defiant expression.

Suddenly, Ilya reaches into his jacket pocket. Cedric steps in front of me.

"Hold on there," he warns.

"What?" Ilya scowls and withdraws a paper sack. He tosses it over Cedric's shoulder to me. "There's a USB stick in there, and the instructions. Forget what I said. I don't want to work with you"—he points at me—"or your friends! You think I want Colin to be a military marine mammal? I was going to try to help you win over my father, but now you can forget it!"

Ilya marches across the yard, back to his pals. Their expressions are in various stages of question marks, but he grabs the ball from one of them and holds it close against his chest while they try to claw it out of his grasp.

I look inside the bag. A USB stick. A sample flyer. And then there is a copy of an article with the heading: "How to Make Your Social Media Account Go Viral." Next to the heading, a note: *My father hates being humiliated. You need the whole world to see Colin and the pod.*

"What is that?" Anna asks, peeking over my shoulder.

"What was he talking about, Sofiya? About working with us?" Petro asks. He pushes his glasses up to the bridge of his nose.

I look at my friends. I have to tell them everything now, don't I?

"It's for the kids' camp and Colin's birthday show. Ilya and I were supposed to . . . build a website. Work on the plans together."

"*Ilya?* At the dolphinarium?" Cedric asks, and I hear the confusion in his voice. "But I thought I was building the website. What does Ilya have to do with this?"

"Yeah? How come we don't know anything about it?" Anna complains.

I sigh. "Because it was part of my punishment . . . for the school fight back in February. It was my tato's idea that Ilya and I work together—"

"Razom!" Petro interrupts.

Anna shoves him a little. "Shut up. This isn't funny."

"I wasn't trying to be funny," he scoffs.

I look over at Ilya.

"And you said nothing? About your punishment?" Cedric asks me quietly. "You took that hit for me?" Then he grins and throws an arm around my shoulders. "You really are my best friend."

"Well, the punishment's over, right? At least you don't have to worry about working with him anymore," Anna says. "And we can get rid of his USB stick."

But I hold up the flyer. "You have to admit—and no offense, Cedric—this is a really good idea."

Anna is peering at the flyer with a critical eye from behind her dark bangs. Petro snatches it from her, then hands it over to Cedric.

He looks up from the paper. "All right. All right. Ilya actually has design skills. I'm still the guy who can write the numbers and program the website, though."

Anna's face twists and she drops her arms to her sides. "Cedric is right."

"We should do this together," Petro says; this time his smile is sly.

"Razom," I agree. "We'll try it."

I glance over at Ilya, surprised to see him watching us. I nod at him, and he pushes himself away from his friends while they try to get him to play ball again.

I think it's better if I tell Ilya after school, when he's alone. I know Ilya well enough to know he won't want a big show about this. But by the way his mouth flicks up, I know he's understood.

He's in. We need him.

CHAPTER 17

Razom

Tato is holding a staff meeting when Cedric, Anna, and Petro arrive and start setting up in the office. I sneak away to the lagoon. I want a moment with Colin. Alone.

The dolphins are gliding through the water, letting out puffs of air. It's quiet, and I approach quietly so that they don't start up a bunch of chatter. Pesyk rolls by and turns on his side, then dives deep down. No bark. No growl. It's like the whole pod knows I want them to be calm.

Lily and Roxi are swimming together, and then Colin pops up in front of me. He just lets out a soft blow.

"Hey there." I lean in and stroke his melon. His whirring is low, like a purr.

"I need you to follow directions, today, okay?" Then in my head, peering into his eye, I add, *I don't know how, but I'm going to find a way to help you. All of you.*

Petro is calling my name. They need help with the passwords. I get up, and the four dolphins are like bowed glass shapes when they break the water's surface.

"Is Ilya coming?" Cedric asks me when I've logged him into

the computer Tato reserved for us. I can tell that the idea of having Ilya around still makes him a little uneasy.

I shrug. "I don't know."

Anna and Petro look at each other.

"What did he say when you asked him?" Petro asks.

"I left it up to him. I told him we were meeting today. But he didn't answer me at all." I did tell him he should come. But Ilya was cold with me when I caught up with him after school.

"Whatever," Anna says. "Let's get to work."

She airdrops us the videos from her phone. We've almost gotten through all of Ilya's USB stick before Tato shows up.

"Someone's looking for you," Tato says.

Ilya steps out from behind him, chewing gum and moping beneath his brown forelock as usual. Tato pats his back and practically shoves him toward the table.

We are all waiting for Ilya to say something. Like maybe a hello. But he goes to the computer and pops his gum.

"What are you doing with my stuff?" he whines.

Cedric frowns.

"Just . . ." I start. "Sit down. I'll show you."

We start to go through the videos, when Ilya says, "We need to reposition the cameras. These are awful angles. They need to be higher up. And the software is terrible."

Tato said something about the angles of the cameras the other day, too, but a bit more nicely. He really wants us kids to do this, but he also said that if we don't do it right, he'll have to go and fix it.

"Fine, Ilya, then what is your suggestion?" I ask.

He reaches for his bag and produces several packages. I pick one up. They're tiny cameras that can be mounted on a magnet.

"U-Spy software. Top-notch stuff," Ilya claims.

"Where did you get these?" Cedric asks, examining one of the packages.

"They're so tiny," Anna says.

"Really cool," Petro mutters. It looks like it pains him to say it.

"Did you steal them?" Cedric asks, rather seriously.

Ilya scoffs. *"No."* Then his cheeks turn a little pink. "They were lying around our house for years. Nobody's ever needed them . . ."

He then shows us his cell phone. "Look, we can set this all up on the U-Spy app. Come on, I'll show you."

We start going through the areas and the pools. Ilya's shoulders seem to soften as we get closer to the dolphins. The pod is in the lagoon, playing with their toys. Each dolphin has a ball, as does Fizz. The sea lions are also playing with some rings. It lightens my mood, too.

"How did you get here?" I whisper to Ilya as he starts to mount the new cameras with magnets and sticky backs.

He shrugs. "I managed to convince my father that you and your dad are training this pod in a really advanced way for this program. And that if I were here, I could keep an eye on it for him. I was bluffing, obviously, but it got him to say yes." He looks me straight in the eyes. "The thing my father hates the most is to be caught by surprise and humiliated in public. With me here, he can feel like he has some control when he actually doesn't."

His stare is so intense that I have to look away. If I decide to believe Ilya, it means I also have to trust him. If someone were to ask me a month ago if that was possible, the answer would have been a definite no. But a lot has changed since then. The Ilya I thought I knew then is not the one I know now.

To my relief, Petro and Cedric call Ilya over to them. He starts showing them where they could get better views of the pools. Ilya's face lights up again as Colin bobs in the water in front of them. If there's one thing I know about Ilya, it's that he genuinely loves these animals. Especially Colin.

I breathe a little easier and walk over to Anna. Roxi tosses a ball onto the platform, and Anna and I bump heads as we bend down to pick it up at the same time.

"Ouch!" I cry.

Anna rubs her head and I hand her the ball to toss. Roxi catches it in her beak and tosses it right back at me.

I glance over at Ilya one more time as he carefully shows the boys how to position the cameras. "Come on," I say to Anna. "Let's go get the pod some ice cubes."

We hurry to the kitchen, and I scoop up a bucket of ice.

"You guys are gonna play with the dolphins while we work?" Cedric complains. His eyes dart over to Ilya with an expression of *Come on. Help me here!*

Anna and I smile at each other.

"We'll meet you downstairs," I say. Because I decide then that I *can* trust Ilya. But also that the technical stuff is too boring. I want to be with the animals.

But Ilya is looking longingly at the bucket.

"Or," I say, "you can all come out to the lagoon and play catch."

The boys look at one another in agreement.

Soon, we're all out on the training stage, all of us laughing. The dolphins swim over, chirping and whirring. Colin clicks at me and I toss him the ball. He swims over with it and uses his beak to toss the ball up to Ilya. Ilya just misses it and forgets to give Colin an ice cube, so Colin responds by shoveling water at Ilya's feet with his head.

We're all laughing. Not Ilya, though. I wonder then if he's taken Colin's prank personally. Ilya scowls down at Colin.

"Come on," I say. I touch Ilya's arm. "He was just joking."

Colin clicks and whirs. He looks like he's smiling. All the dolphins do.

"He's laughing with you, not at you," I say.

Ilya finally drops an ice cube down his beak and this time, when Colin tosses him the ball, Ilya catches it and Colin rises out of the water and claps his flippers.

Even Ilya is laughing now.

Ilya then suggests we reposition the cameras in the experimental pool. "You can show me what you've been practicing," he adds.

But first, we have to wait until the U-Spy app is uploaded onto my phone. We adjust the new cameras until Ilya is happy with them. It takes a while, and by the time we're done, Tato joins us and says it's okay to call Colin into the pool.

Colin pops up at the rim and Ilya reaches out, like a reflex, to pat his melon. For a second, I feel a flash of envy. Ilya might have his own relationship with Colin now, but I can't think of anything on this earth that's stronger than the bond Colin and I have. I look the wise dolphin in the eye then and it feels like we're staring into each other's souls.

Ready to practice sign language? I say with my eyes.

I can tell that Colin understands by the way he pulls away from Ilya and nods his head.

A few minutes later, I'm in the pool with Anna as Ilya gets his camera ready to make a video. Cedric and Petro are prepared to give the hand signals.

"Watch this," I call to Ilya, then nod to Cedric. He pulls down his blindfold and begins. "Colin has to do the commands in the right order."

"Fetch, person, board," Cedric shouts and signs at the same time. "Swim through hoop!"

Colin swims over to where I'm floating on my back and picks me up in the water. I let out a little whoop as he carries me to the surfboard. Then, as I float on the board, I watch Colin swim to the hoop and dive through. He's completed both tasks perfectly!

Everyone claps, including Ilya.

I look at Colin, beaming with pride as he collects his reward.

Anna and I reposition ourselves and Cedric signals again. "Fetch, board, person."

First, Colin swims to Anna, but curves past her to fetch the surfboard. Anna is closest to the board this time, and he brings it to her.

Cheers echo through the pool area. They're seeing now what I've always known—that Colin is capable of understanding so much more than what people might think. But he can do more than understand. He can solve problems, too.

I look down at the bottom of the pool. There's a deflated hoop that's resting at the bottom. Which means Colin wouldn't be able to swim through it.

"Petro," I say. "Ask Colin to swim through the sunken hoop down there."

Petro looks confused but does what's asked of him.

"Swim! Through! Hoop!" Petro says, signaling to Colin with his hands.

Colin dives down while we all watch on the underwater camera monitor that Tato installed a long time ago. Everyone seems to hold their breath.

Colin begins to touch the hoop with his beak until it starts to float up. He noses it higher and higher toward the surface. Finally, when the hoop is up high enough, Colin swims through it.

We are screaming!

Ilya smiles broadly. "That was so cool! *So* cool!"

He and Cedric and Petro give one another high fives. I never thought I'd see the day Ilya and Cedric would get along like this.

I climb out of the water with Anna. I want to show Ilya something else. Something I've been teaching Colin for a while now. I pull down the bandanna from my head over my eyes and lift my finger. I hear Colin cackling.

Open! Gate! Fetch! Pod! I signal. I whip off the bandanna and watch.

Colin dives under the water and we can see, on the monitor, that he is heading for the gate. Tato has installed a button that Colin now can use from the inside only. He throws the gate open and swims out into the main pool. I turn to Ilya. "I taught him that." We all wait to see if Colin will actually bring the rest of the pod.

Soon enough, all four dolphins are gliding in from the main pool to claim their rewards. Ilya, Cedric, and the twins are cheering and congratulating the pod as they feed them their ice cubes. But Colin swims straight to me. I bend down and pass my hand over his rubbery melon. He nudges his rostrum into my palm, where he likes to be petted the most.

"Good boy," I say, beaming.

Tato quiets us down. "This seems to be working really well. I think we'll be ready for those camps and the big event by May. Now, you guys have to get to work and start building up that audience and registration." He looks at me. "I'm really proud of you, Sofiya. The dolphinarium in Hawaii will be ecstatic with my report. They're going to get so much international attention."

I feel the back of my neck get hot, embarrassed by Tato's enthusiastic praise. Ilya looks away from me, his brow creased, and scuffs his foot on the tiles.

"All right," Tato calls. "Let's get them all out of here."

I smile and nod. "Colin!"

Colin whirs and clicks.

I hold up my finger. "Open! Gate! Pod! Run!" I say and sign.

He chirps for a second, then swims away. We all bend over the rim, but Colin swims around the whole pod, and the next thing we know, one after the other, they are all leaving the experimental pool.

Tato shakes his head and grasps my shoulder, but he is smiling. "I was kidding when I suggested that idea," he says. And we look at each other, both remembering his joke about teaching Colin to run away from Major Chaban. I glance nervously at Ilya. I don't want him to know that's where it came from.

Anna and I get showered and dressed. We all meet back at the office and use the rest of the day to get the video, photos, and messaging ready for our social media pages. Each of us has a job. And now that Ilya is here, the video editing moves faster than ever. Today's video is excellent and we upload it to Telegram, Instagram, and our new Facebook page and Twitter account.

Ilya has even put the video to music, and included a surprise ending with all of us together while Colin jumps into the air and tosses a ball right at the camera before the camp registration's pop-up screen appears.

Almost immediately, our video starts garnering likes and follows!

"Look." Petro points at the Twitter feed. "The dolphinarium in Odesa is following us now, too."

"Hey, everyone! *Klassno!*" Cedric cries. "Miss Yvette's following our Instagram and our Facebook page!"

Smiling, I walk over to Ilya and extend my hand. "Congratulations," I say. "You did it."

He doesn't take my hand at first, and I wave it at him. "Do you know what this means? Accept my hand," I say.

"I guess I forgive you. For assuming I had something more sinister in my pocket yesterday," he says.

I give him a nod and we shake on it.

"Is what your father says true? That the dolphins could become . . . I don't know . . . better known around the world?"

I shrug. "I guess. Why?"

He shakes his head. "I don't know. Never mind." He then shows me his phone. "Listen, with the app, you can watch the video cameras from home."

"Watch the dolphins sleep, that is?" I tease.

"No." He frowns. "I mean you can if you . . . Wait. How *do* they sleep?"

"Easy. They use their two brain halves. They sleep with one eye closed, and half their brain is awake. Then they close their other eye—"

"Get out of here," Ilya says and punches me lightly on the shoulder.

"I'm serious." And I am, but Cedric suddenly squeals again, his hands palming his cheeks.

"Look at this!" Cedric points at the computer. "We're already booked up for the first camp and half for the second week!"

None of us can believe it. We're all standing behind him, looking over his shoulder, but there it is. We've got fifteen participants for the first week, and they are all paid! And we've got seven so far for the second week!

We all laugh as Petro dances around, chanting, "*Ra-zom! Ra-zom! Ra-zom!*"

Ilya can't hide his smile through his scowl, and claps Petro on the shoulder, laughing.

Outside, the sun has already gone down, though none of us noticed the time. We are all quickly putting our coats on when Anna's and Petro's cell phones go off. Their mom likes to call them at the same time on Telegram.

"*Allo? Mam?*" Anna says first. "We're listening."

Anna's forehead wrinkles and she looks at Petro. Petro pushes his glasses up and sniffs, nodding into his phone.

"All right, Mama," he says. "We're coming now."

Anna's face falls when she hangs up. "My dad has been

released from the base. But only because he's been stripped of his military status."

"What does that mean?" Cedric asks.

My look darts to Ilya. His face is stony.

"It means their dad doesn't have a job any longer," he says.

The five of us look at one another. All of a sudden, the room is illuminated from the outside. We're blinded by beams of light cutting in through the office window. I put my hand up to shade my eyes and peer out.

"Tato!" I scream. "Tato!"

Outside, in the parking lot, a line of military trucks. And the shape of Major Chaban. Six men with rifles are marching behind him straight to our front doors.

CHAPTER 18

Checkmate

Ilya looks at me, frightened. "Sofiya—"

"He can't." I shake my head. "Your father can't do this!"

In the foyer, we can hear three of the dolphinarium staff shouting over Major Chaban's gruff commands.

"What is going on?" my tato demands over and over.

I go out into the foyer. Petro, Anna, and Cedric follow close behind me. I don't check whether Ilya is coming. I don't know what to think.

Everyone is pointing fingers at the other party. Major Chaban is holding a sheaf of papers in his hand. He thrusts them at my father. The six military guards are blocking the entrance. Each of them is holding an assault rifle. When they see us kids, they look surprised. One of them moves toward us.

"Who are you?" he asks.

I want to run away. It feels like a thousand needles are raining on my skin, but just then, Tato shoves past Major Chaban and steps between us and the guard.

"This is my daughter. You step away now."

Tato herds us away from the guards and that's when I realize that Ilya hasn't even come out of the office. I whirl around and immediately understand: Ilya's hiding something. Did he know this was going to happen? But why is he hiding from Major Chaban now?

"We've discussed this long enough," Major Chaban says to Tato and the staff. He wiggles his fingers. "The keys."

All the guards shift and stiffen, as if he's just given them the command to arrest us.

With chills running down my back, I watch as Tato reaches into his trouser pocket and pulls out the key ring. He removes a set of keys for the building and hands them over. I stare at them in Major Chaban's hand.

"Tato, you can't!" I start, but Major Chaban's glare roots me to my spot.

"The dolphinarium is now the property of the Russian Federation," he says, as if this explanation makes sense. "Oleksandr Antonovych, as I've said, you and your staff members now have a choice. Some of you can apply to keep your jobs—maybe—as sea mammal trainers, but only if you agree to take part in repurposing them for the military program."

"No!" I cry. "Tato! You promised! You promised this wouldn't happen!"

Major Chaban sneers at me. "Then that was really silly of him."

I back into Tato. Cedric, Anna, and Petro move closer to me.

"So, Oleksandr, what do you say? Are you prepared to meet my terms or do you want to pack up and leave?"

Tato folds his arms, and, like Babushka, he presses his lips really tight until, for a moment, they go white. His jaw is twitching. "And if I don't agree to work for you?"

I look wildly at him, then at Major Chaban. If my father abandons the animals, then those thugs with assault rifles will be responsible for them. I can't bear the thought of abandoning the pod and Fizz. The sea lions!

"You have to stay!" I croak to Tato.

Major Chaban chides, "Yes, Oleksandr Antonovych, you should stay. But you will no longer be the manager." He sweeps his arm over the other staff. "In fact, anyone who stays will have to agree to work under military command. Because this facility will be phased into a military base over the next months."

Tato looks at both me and Ilya's father. "Can I think about it?"

The major shrugs. I can't tell what he wants my tato's decision to be. "Go ahead. You have twenty-four hours."

Major Chaban turns on his heel and waves for the guards to follow him. My blood chills when I see that he's heading for Tato's office, the keys rattling in his hand.

Tato takes me by the shoulder and beckons to the other

kids. "Come on. Let's go. There's nothing more we can do here right now."

"No," I say again, but this time it's a whimper.

I look over my shoulder, just waiting for Major Chaban to exclaim surprise when he sees Ilya inside. But there is nothing, and Tato shoves us out the door.

Outside, I'm shivering.

"Are you cold?" Tato asks. The rest of the employees come silently out, their faces pale beneath the streetlamp.

"No," I say. But my teeth are chattering.

"Sofiya, it's okay. I'll think of something." He turns to my friends. I'm still looking for some sign of Ilya. Some sign that it can't be true.

"Are you kids hungry?" Tato asks. "I'll buy you tacos at Ivan's."

Cedric, Anna, and Petro all shake their heads and make their excuses. I'm not really listening. Anna comes over and puts an arm around my shoulders.

"What's going to happen?" she asks. "To my father? To the dolphins? To Sevastopol?"

"What's going to happen if my tato decides not to come back?" I say in a whisper. Tears spring into my eyes.

Petro is also close to me, and his eyes are wide. We're all frightened.

“I can ask whether my father knows anything,” he offers. “About how we might help.”

But it doesn’t make me feel any better. Petro and Anna’s tato now has his own livelihood to think about.

Tato tries to calm his staff at the side of the building. But I see the adults’ faces. They all look defeated, as if they’ve given up hope.

“We’ll see you tomorrow at school,” Cedric says.

My friends leave me after another round of hugs.

Tato sends his staff, his former staff, on their way and beckons to me. We walk toward the promenade in silence. He reaches out to put a hand on my shoulder, but I duck away. I am angry! *So* angry! What is there to think about? He *has* to stay with the pod! He promised me he would have a plan!

“Where did Ilya go?” I ask then.

“I don’t know,” Tato says. It’s the only answer anyone seems to have to any question. Everything is a mess. It’s mass chaos!

The streetlamps make small pools of light. The tide is whispering against the shore as it comes in and rolls out. In the cove, the waves shake up the pebbles like a box of marbles. In the distance, the lights of ships and tankers blink. We’re only a little ways away from Ivan’s—I can already smell the frying fish—when someone steps away from the seawall.

"Ilya?" My anger rises again.

Tato stops. Ilya looks down, his face in shadow.

"Hey," Tato says. But his voice is deep, a warning. "What are you doing here?"

"It's my fault," Ilya says.

"What is?" Tato and I ask in unison.

Ilya speaks really fast. "I was telling the truth. I did ask my father if I could come back after we talked yesterday. Because I *really* wanted to be here. I wanted to help. But he caught me watching your Instagram videos. About the sign language. And that's when he got the idea for the cameras. He made me come back and—"

"What?" Tato breathes quietly.

"He said he wanted the cameras repositioned so that he could—"

"Spy on us," Tato says with disbelief. "He asked you to position a camera in the office, didn't he? Where our staff was going over finances. Your father sent you so that he could get the information he needed to take the dolphinarium out from under us."

I am frozen to my spot, ice-cold. Tato coughs into his fist, turns, and walks away.

My hands are clenched deep inside my coat pockets.

Ilya scuffs the pavement with his shoe, his head hung low.

"I didn't know that he was planning to move this quickly. I thought I had time. And it was the only way . . ." he says really, really quietly.

"Only way for what?"

He looks up. Tears roll down his face. "It was the only way I'd be able to see Colin again. It was the only way I could get back to the dolphinarium. But, Sofiya—"

"No," I say, my palms up. I back away. "No, no, no. I'm not listening to you. You could have said no. You could have told me. We could have stopped him. But you just went ahead and hung up the cameras."

"He only asked me to reposition one of your dad's cameras in the office. He doesn't know about the U-Spy cameras. That we have the app," Ilya cries at my back.

I spin around. Tato is waiting up ahead, impatiently calling my name, but I stop and turn back to Ilya.

"What are you talking about?" I ask.

"He doesn't know that you can watch the dolphins from home . . . and make videos."

I frown. "So what? Your father just seized the entire dolphinarium! He won't need the cameras! And what point is there in making videos for a camp that will never exist, for a pod of dolphins that I might not ever be able to see again? *My* pod." I look him straight in the eyes. "You took them away from me."

“Sofiya. Let’s go,” Tato calls up ahead.

I turn away, my heart sinking further and further with each step that I take away from Colin.

Tato and I walk over the promenade. We stop at the food truck, though Ivan is winding down for the night. He hands out free strong coffee to the lingering men in the park, then invites us inside the caravan to eat. When the food truck is shut up tight, all three dogs gather around me at the narrow, wobbly table and wiggle for attention. Tato gives Ivan the long, drawn-out story about Major Chaban and the dolphinarium. I’m too tired to add to it. Too tired, and too sad.

“It’s a strategic invasion,” Ivan says ominously when Tato is finished. He hands me a warm salmon taco and a lemonade. He delivers a poke bowl for Tato. “The Russians are moving in and not only into Crimea.”

He takes a seat across from me and wipes his long mustache with the back of his hand. His eyes are light gray, but they’re on fire. His coffee is so strong I can taste it just from the smell.

“I got reports that there are insurgents in the east. In Donbas. In Luhansk . . .” He looks at Tato knowingly and smacks his mouth.

“What are insurgents?” I ask.

Ivan narrows his eyes at me, his knee bouncing. “Men who

are fighting for Russia in Ukraine. They can be soldiers sent from Russia, like here in Crimea, or they can be Russians who are living and working here in Ukraine and decide to help Russia take our land."

"Just like Major Chaban taking the dolphinarium," Tato adds.

"And Ilya," I say. A tear springs into my eye but I wipe it angrily away.

"That might be more complicated than you think," Tato says quietly, but Ivan sniffs and rolls his eyes.

"Can't trust any of them," he says. "What are you going to do, Oleksandr? About the dolphinarium?"

Tato winces and glances over at me. "I've got twenty-four hours. I have a lot of phone calls to make tomorrow."

Ivan sniffs again and gives my dad that knowing look once more. "We are not going to let Russkyi mir into our borderlands."

Russkyi mir . . . the Russian world. It's not a nice thing to say. It means violence, and blood, and criminality, and corruption. Miss Yvette once said Russkyi mir involves having our Ukrainian language, our culture, our traditions all taken away, along with our land.

"There are Russians who don't want Ukrainians to exist," she'd said.

Ivan is watching me then. He points a long finger. "Don't forget who you are, Sofiya."

Tato tips his head. "She's doesn't, Ivan. She's both."

Ivan wipes a hand down his mustache. "Both. Pickle in the middle, is that it? Well, Oleksandr, she'll have to choose soon." Ivan stands up now, his long braided hair swinging between his shoulders. His mouth is set in a determined line. "We aren't going to let them do that, are we?" He looks pointedly at my father, who melts a little under his stare.

"No," Tato says softly. "We won't."

Tato and I eat in silence. Marble lays his head on my knee and wags his tail. With a groan, Musk lays down next to me. Monk, begging for a piece of fish, puts a paw on Tato's thigh. He pets the dog absentmindedly.

"Well," Ivan says before picking up our empty plates, "I have a feeling that Major Chaban is about to call checkmate. Unless you can make a move that he's not thinking of."

In chess, when someone calls checkmate, it means the king is threatened with capture. There is no possible escape.

"What *is* your next move?" I ask Tato. "You can't just give up!"

But Tato gives Ivan a look of acceptance, the same one he gives when he quits a game, which is the etiquette in chess. If you can't win, you call quits. But the dolphins—Colin, Pesyk, Roxi, and Lily—they're not chess pieces. They're our family.

"What are *you* going to do, Ivan Markovych?" my father suddenly asks.

Ivan swaggers over like the Cossack that he is. He throws the dish rag onto the table like a challenge to a duel. He raises one eyebrow and looks sternly down at my tato.

"I'll pack up this rust bucket. That's what I'll do. I'll pack this place up, drive over the land bridge, and go fight out east. Like any Ukrainian worth his weight should do."

He winks and rubs the top of my head.

I think he's trying to tell my tato that he'd give up everything.

Everything has already been taken from me. And I'd do anything to get it back.

CHAPTER 19

Queen of Hearts

The next morning, I get up at the first sound of someone in the kitchen. Neptune dashes into my room and snakes around my ankles before I can come out. I expect to find Tato in the kitchen, but it's Babushka.

"Good morning," she says. And I can tell by the way her eyes are pitying me that she's heard the news. She puts a finger to her lips.

"Where's Tato?"

"Still sleeping. He called me last night."

I slump against the kitchen counter. "Did he tell you that Ilya lied? That he's behind this, too?"

Babushka clicks her tongue and tilts her head. "You children . . . You have no . . . Did he tell you why?"

"He said it was so he could see Colin," I say in a hushed whisper.

Babushka's eyes get big. "Well! That's a start!"

"A start for what?" I demand.

"Seems like you won him over. You or Colin and the other dolphins."

"Won him over?"

"Kotyku, don't you see? You helped him feel something. He cares about the dolphins."

"No, he clearly doesn't. If he did, he wouldn't have let this happen."

She sighs and props her elbows on the counter next to me, staring at me. "Remember when I told you about how all animals have the ability to communicate with any other animal?"

I nod.

Babushka looks thoughtful. "I wasn't only talking about critters, I was talking about humans, too. I told you to listen with your eyes, not only your ears. Everyone wants to be understood. Never doubt that. Most of all, though"—she taps the left side of her chest—"we have to listen with the heart. It seems to me his heart might be conflicted."

I blow a raspberry and shake my head. "He's no different than his father. He manipulated me and my friends."

"Did he, now?" She takes out her cell phone, taps a few things on the screen, then shows it to me.

When I look over at it, I recognize our Telegram account for the kids' camp. @IlIl_squared—that's Ilya's profile—has uploaded our last video, and it has over ten *thousand* views! *Thousands* of comments. My mouth drops.

"Swipe to the next video," Babushka says.

I do. And I am speechless. Ilya has also posted a video of all of us in the foyer. The six soldiers. Major Chaban waving the sheaf of papers at Tato. Me and my friends, huddled and scared.

There is a caption:

The dolphinarium is now part of the Russian Federation and will be handed over to the navy. Any civilians who once benefited from the dolphins, used them for treatment or rehabilitation, will no longer have access to Colin, Pesyk, Lily, Roxi, or Fizz, the Beluga whale. The Communicate with Colin program will also be canceled! The world has to know what the Russian military is planning to do!

There are lines and lines of hashtags. Ilya has tagged a bunch of people and organizations as well, including Miss Yvette.

That's weird, I think. I'd never imagined him—or anyone in 6C—having had a relationship with Miss Yvette like we did. And then I think of Tato, and how Ilya always blooms under his attention . . .

I glance at the reactions. There are hundreds of sad emojis, angry emojis, open-mouthed emojis on this post. The comments are angry and outraged. But Miss Yvette has posted a thumbs-up, and then a comment:

You have learned well, Ilya. This is how to bring attention to an issue.

Dazed, I hand Babushka the phone back.

"Ilya's going to get into so much trouble," I say. Assuming Major Chaban knows who IlIl_squared is.

Babushka nods, and taps her heart again. "That is likely very true. If I were you, I'd say he's pretty darned brave." Babushka taps her heart again. "I think it's time for you to become the Queen of Hearts."

I'm still reeling from this when Tato walks in. His hair is down to his shoulders, and he needs to shave.

"What's going on?" he asks.

Babushka hands him the phone. I watch him, but his face is set in a grim expression. He sighs and shakes his head.

"I don't know what this should do. It's only going to make my job a lot harder."

Neptune meow-growls for his food, and Babushka pops open a can. He jogs over to her and she sets his bowl down, where he makes wet cat-eating noises. I watch Tato.

"So, you're going to stay on? You'll stay with the dolphinarium?" I say.

He scratches his head. "I have a lot of phone calls to make, Sofiya. And you need to get to school."

"But, Tato, we've got a full camp for both weeks now. I checked the website. Both weeks are full. With payments in. Please, we need to convince Major Chaban somehow to at least let us go through with the program. And Colin's birthday. Please!"

He frowns and makes his huffing sounds. "The birthday? Are you kidding me? It's the last thing anyone is thinking of."

I stamp my foot. I can't take this. He's not even going to try. I run into my room and slam the door. I throw myself on my stomach and cover my head with my pillow. I can still hear their voices: Babushka's and Tato's. They're not raised, but they're loud. I don't care. When Tato makes up his mind, it's really hard to change it.

There's a soft knock at the door and I stiffen, pulling the covers over me. "Go away."

"Sofiya."

Just like I thought, it's Tato. I hear the door open. Neptune springs onto my bed, where he starts kneading the covers. I stay still and don't disturb the cat when he lays down between my calves.

Tato is there. I can feel him on the far side of my room. I peek out from beneath the pillow and see that he is looking at my drawings strung up along the wall. I duck back under.

"You're just as good as she was," he says. "You inherited your mother's talent. Maybe even better."

I hear paper rustling, and then sense something has changed.

Again, I peek out. This time I sit up, careful not to bother Neptune as I slide my legs out from beneath him. Tato's found the hidden picture of my mother on the bus, the bird's-eye view of her abandoning me.

He carefully unclips it, and my heart stands still. He turns to me. "Sofi—"

"If you don't stay with the animals," I accuse him, "I'm going to die. I'll never forgive you for this. You might as well just send me to Moscow to be with my mother, because I'll never forgive you."

Tato's face crumples.

"I don't even know where she is in Moscow," he says. "Do you know how big Moscow is?"

"I don't care. I'll find her. I've got almost enough saved to buy a bus ticket."

"A bus ticket? Sofiya, if I had a chance to put you in touch with your mother, do you not believe I would?"

"Why would you? You hate her. And she's Russian. You'll hate her even more now!"

Tato drops his arms to his sides. "I don't, though. Sofiya, it makes me so sad that you think I do. I never hated her."

"Why not?" I scream. "Why don't you? At least I'd know why she left!"

Neptune, startled, jumps off the bed. Tato sinks onto the mattress in the cat's spot, the drawing in his lap.

"It doesn't work that way. We can't choose who to fall in love with, but we can make the decision to love them every day. Even the hard ones. I promised to love her. And I always will. My goodness, Sofiya. She gave me you!"

He reaches for my hands and I let him take them. He looks down at them and strokes my palms. "Even when she was at her absolute worst, I loved your mother, Sofiya. I think that is what drove her away. After Ilya fell out of the boat and she wasn't able to save his mother—her best friend . . ." He sighs heavily. "She hated *herself* so much . . . She *wanted* everyone to hate her, too. We all still loved her. Of course we did. But she couldn't accept that."

I can't see anything. The tears are blinding me.

He sighs again. "Major Chaban did not make things easier . . . He never forgave her, for something that was never her fault to begin with. He never . . . he never put the blame where it was due."

I wipe my tears. "What do you mean?"

But Tato closes his eyes and shakes his head. "Some people just refuse to accept their part in a problem. It's easier to blame everyone and everything else."

I still don't understand, but Tato pulls me in for a hug. It feels good.

"I'm going to try, Sofiya. I'm going to stay with the dolphins if at all possible," he says. "You're right. We can't abandon those we love. I'll do what I have to in order to protect them."

"Me too," I say.

But right now, I don't even know where to begin.

CHAPTER 20

Forbidden

When I wake up the next morning, my first thought is that last night had to have been a nightmare. Major Chaban can't possibly be in charge of the dolphinarium. Of *my* pod. How can this be real?

But when I get to school, things continue to get worse and worse.

Cedric waves at me with both arms to hurry up. It's warmer out and I'm hot from the ride. I lock up my bike and pull off my beanie. Rumors float around about an emergency assembly.

On my way to English, I come around the corner and run into Cedric and the twins. Petro and Anna are as white as ghosts, though.

"What is going on—?"

Just then, the speakers squeak like chalk against a blackboard and someone spits into the microphone. A man's voice sounds in Ukrainian: *"Uvaha! Uvaha!"* Attention! Attention!

"It's Director Vovk," Cedric says.

"All students are to go to the gymnasium for a special

announcement. I repeat, all students are to go straight to the gymnasium for a special announcement."

Cedric and Petro pick up their bags first, and I put an arm around Anna's shoulder.

"Are you going to be okay? How's your tato?"

Anna shakes her head and shrugs. "Tato is okay. He told us that everyone who brought them food while they were under siege are now on a list with the Russians. Including my mom."

"And our brother, Denys, was arrested," Petro says. He sounds as if he might cry.

"Arrested for *what*?" I ask. I know that Denys is just finishing up at polytechnic college. He's always been so nice to us kids—giving us rides to places like the beach or the mall.

Cedric whips out his cell phone and waves it at me. "For posting on Twitter. The police geolocated him."

I look at Anna, who now frowns and says angrily, "He posted a video of himself and his friends driving around Sevastopol the other night, singing the Ukrainian anthem."

My mouth forms into a big, round O. I can hardly get out a reply. "They . . . the police arrested him because he was singing the national anthem?" My heart is racing. "A list?"

"For being provocateurs," Petro says.

I remember the "special department" where provocateurs

go, the one the journalists were asking the little green men about.

Anna points to herself and Petro. "Our whole family is on that list now."

I shudder.

We've arrived at the front doors of the gymnasium, waiting to get inside, when I see Ilya and the Idiots up ahead and feel betrayed all over again. His friends are waving their arms and jumping up and down, making a bunch of noise. But not Ilya. I narrow my eyes at the back of his head and hope he feels my daggers.

The gymnasium is chaos as we try to find seats. All the teachers are up front. Miss Yvette has her arms wrapped around herself, her hair done up high in a scarf. She gazes around but doesn't seem to be looking at anything. Someone says something to her and she barely turns her head, only nods, and takes a step back. She blends into the thick line of teachers.

Mr. Vovk walks in. Tall, thin, wearing that brown suit and blue tie. His brows are raised halfway up his head as he claps and nods at various groups and tells them to quiet down. Finally, he goes to the microphone located under the left basketball hoop.

He taps it and we cover our ears as it squeals.

"Good morning, students," Mr. Vovk says into the microphone. This time, he's speaking in Russian.

Miss Yvette raises her chin and I wave, but she doesn't appear to see us.

"We have an announcement to make," Mr. Vovk continues in Russian. "As decreed by the Russian Federation, you will all be released from school for the spring holidays in a week, as planned. However, beginning today, you will turn in all of your textbooks, all homework, and all tests—all school materials—to your teachers."

I look at Cedric, Anna, and Petro. All the students stare around the room, confused. We have exams and quizzes coming up and need those textbooks to study.

He continues, still in Russian. "You will receive new textbooks and materials starting today. Teachers are instructed to begin phasing out the old books and materials and using the new ones for the remainder of this school year. Upon your return from spring break, all classes, all teachers, and all students will use only the Russian language to teach and to speak in. Ukrainian will no longer be the language of this school."

A lot of students are talking now. Petro and I look at each other and I hoarsely cry, "*Ni!*" No!

"It's our language!" I shout to the audience. "*Mova! Tse . . .*" But I can't finish the slogan because I choke on the lump in my throat. *It's our only weapon!*

Then Petro whips off his glasses. "Ni!" he shouts in Ukrainian, too.

Anna and Cedric start chanting "No!" in Ukrainian as well. Some of the kids behind us join in, but as Mr. Vovk's eyes pass over the entire gymnasium, our voices get weaker and weaker.

His jowls are hanging lower than usual. "Allowances to transition will be given next week only. All teachers and administrators—all students—will return from the break prepared to deal with the curricula in Russian. You are now excused!"

Miss Yvette turns on her heel, her arms still wrapped around herself. But as she heads out the door, I see our biology teacher put a hand on her shoulder and jerk his head in the opposite direction of her class. She drops her arms and follows him instead.

"Come on," I say. "Let's get to class."

But ten minutes later, Miss Yvette still hasn't shown up. Kids start talking louder the longer we're left without a teacher.

"Stay quiet, everyone," I say.

"I don't understand you," Antonin taunts. "Speak Russian!"

"Shut up," I say in Russian and put my hands on my hips. "Did you understand *that*?"

But the class continues their chatting.

"Stay quiet," I repeat, "and nobody will come to check on

us." I stare Antonin down, and he seems to understand that it's a good idea.

Cedric, Anna, Petro, and I huddle in the far corner, where I'm finally able to tell them about how Ilya betrayed us. How he admitted that his father made him remount the cameras to be able to spy on my tato and his staff. How he claimed that he did it to be back at the dolphinarium and working with Colin.

"He can't be trusted," Anna says sharply.

Petro pinches the bridge of his nose and sighs. "Nope, he's not to be trusted."

Cedric looks away, disappointed. "Man, I was starting to think he was cool."

"But there's more," I say, showing them my cell phone. "The other thing he told me was that his father doesn't know anything about the U-Spy cameras. That I can still watch the videos with the app. I didn't think it would be any use when he first told me. But I think Ilya mounted more cameras than we realized."

Cedric's eyes bulge. "Whoa."

I start up the app as Petro and Anna peer over my shoulder. It gives me a choice as to which cameras I can view. Suddenly, there is a moving image of my tato—I recognize the red T-shirt he had on this morning. But he's with someone else, too.

"That's Major Chaban," Cedric says in wonder. "Can you get sound, too?"

Petro moves his thumb over the volume adjuster. "Holy moly," he says. Another one of Miss Yvette's favorite lines.

I look up toward the door to see if she's come in, but we're still teacherless.

My friends line up behind me to watch the screen on my phone. They're in Tato's office. I get chills down my legs and arms. Major Chaban is sitting in my tato's chair. Tato hands him a folder.

"These are all the actual figures, and the business concept that my *daughter* has come up with," Tato says.

"A business concept?" Major Chaban looks directly up at the camera. "She managed that in the last twelve hours?"

"That's the clock," I say quietly. "He's looking at the clock."

"Did Ilya hang it up last—" Cedric starts, but I wave at him to shut up.

"No," Tato says. "It's something we've been working on for some time now. As you *must* know."

Ilya's father glances up and flips through the pages. "It doesn't matter."

"That's what I thought you would say," Tato says. "That you would find something wrong with the entire idea. That doesn't matter. But *this* does." Tato hands his cell phone to Major

Chaban. "If you look at the number of responses to yesterday's videos, I think you'll see that the whole world is watching."

Major Chaban looks at the phone, then brings it closer to his face. "What am I looking at here?"

"Two things. A very popular social media account that's been following our dolphins and is garnering worldwide attention. That video has been shared by our research partners in the United States, in Mexico, in Odesa and Kharkiv, in Romania . . . And not only on Twitter but on Facebook, on Instagram, and on Telegraph."

I groan and shake my phone. "Telegram, Tato! Telegram!"

But he's not listening, of course, because he can't hear me.

"And number two," Tato continues. "There is a waiting list of now three hundred kids for our special program, Communicate with Colin."

"Three hundred—!" all my friends shout in unison.

"Hey! What's going on over there?" Antonin calls.

Vova stands up from his desk, craning his neck.

Anna pushes herself away, but I hardly notice, because I'm focused on Major Chaban. He drops Tato's phone on the desk and I wince. If I toss his phone like that, Tato has a fit.

"And?"

"And . . ." Tato takes a step to Major Chaban. "Let's stop the charade, shall we?"

Major Chaban's back straightens. "I don't know what you mean," he says, dryly.

I bring the phone closer to my ear as the classroom gets louder. Anna is somehow riling the kids up on the other side of the room.

"I know what this is about." Tato takes another step closer to Major Chaban. "You want to keep tearing me and my family down. But I know one thing. You are always blaming everyone else for your miseries. You blamed *my* wife for *your* wife's accident. You diverted attention away from what *you* did on that day. Well, you got what you wanted, right? You got the whole town talking about my wife, my Natalia's faults, and how she was irresponsible. When it was *you* who was driving the boat. *You* panicked. Not her. Elena was screaming at you to slow down."

Major Chaban springs from his chair, and I almost drop the phone. He leans on his desk; I can see his chest expanding and deflating like he's just finished a run.

"What?" Tato leans in as well. "I have lost nearly everything. But I'm grateful for what I have left. What I don't understand is you. Isn't it enough that your accusations left Sofiya without a mother in her life? Me, without my wife? But you! You have a son! And you have forgotten about him in all of this . . . That boy needs his father. That boy needs your love!" Tato picks up the folder and waves it. "Our kids created this business plan *together*. Your son. My daughter. And in less than twenty-four hours, the registrations for these day camps are bringing in enough to pay the rent on two months."

"*What?*" Major Chaban snatches the file. "Two months? How is that possible?"

"And if we held these camps over the whole summer, we'd probably be able to pay rent for half a year. That is, if the day camps we already have planned go well. The business plan is all there."

Major Chaban looks at the pages. It takes excruciatingly long. He sinks back into the chair. I keep looking up, but Anna and Petro are now over with the other kids, huddled together. Cedric is still next to me, as riveted as I am.

"This is what I'm going to do," Major Chaban finally says. "You can hold the camps. Hold this ridiculous birthday show. But after that, we will be phasing this into a new training base and the animals will belong to the Russian navy."

"Yeah, Tato!" I squeal, though I can't help but shudder at the second half of Major Chaban's conditions. At the very least, this will buy us some time.

Anna and Petro rush over.

"I told the class the whole story," Anna says.

I look over at my classmates of 6A. Larissa and Vova are looking at me, nodding.

"Anything you need, Sofiya, you let us know," Larissa says before more and more kids begin asking me questions about the camps.

The bell rings. Our class is over. And it isn't until I'm sitting in biology that I wonder what ever happened to Miss Yvette.

CHAPTER 21

Stopping Time

Everything is different. Everything. Tato's on the phone a lot. Babushka paces our living room, listening to the news. Every time I go to the dolphinarium, my heart skips and my stomach hurts. Yes, I have time with the pod. Yes, we've gotten the green light for the camps, but I remember an incident on the Black Sea a few summers ago. A boy in an air tube, the kind parents give their kids so that they can float, was bobbing in the waves, his parents involved with their smaller child. Nobody noticed that the boy's tube had a leak in it, except Tato, who went out there and steered the boy back to safety.

"He was slowly sinking," he'd reported to the mother.

That's how I feel. I feel like we are sinking.

The night before the kids' camps are supposed to begin, Tato is ahead of me and turns off the lights. He hasn't noticed that I'm not behind him as he grabs the door handle to the kitchen and yanks it open. A bright slice of light illuminates the dark space before the door falls shut, the last of the light gone with it.

I hear the soft puffs of air from the dolphins, the water rippling with their movements and lapping against the basin. I hear the longer blow from Fizz. The sea lions next door have also quieted down. Then there is a distinctly louder water sound near me, and a soft chirp.

I don't need to see Colin to know it's him, or where to find him.

I kneel down and my hand goes over his melon. He's moving, nudging my elbow with his snout, like he wants to play. He's not done for the night. He wants more attention. He's excited, but not in a good way. He must be feeling the differences, too.

I'm not excited about tomorrow either. The clock is ticking, and after these camps, nobody really knows how we're going to help the pod, how we're going to save them from becoming the property of the Russian navy.

But I'm not ready to call checkmate.

"See you tomorrow, Colin," I say. And I walk out, blinded by the bright industrial lights, and my tears.

The next day, the first day of the camps, I wait as all twenty participants pile in, excited, chattering. I see Larissa and she waves, but I don't wave back.

Tato greets them with his smile. I know I'm sulking, and I can't help it.

We have so many extra participants because Major Chaban forced us to make the groups bigger despite Tato's protests that it will stress the animals.

So, now, there are four kids for each dolphin and for Fizz. The sea lions put up a fuss when Anna, Petro, Cedric, and I walk into the staging area to present the overview of the week. The kids are clapping and Tato introduces us as the Communicate with Colin leaders in this program. We're the kids here for the kids.

The participants are all around our age, a couple are older. Even Denys, Petro and Anna's brother, who was released from the police station with a bogus traffic fine, is there to watch. Anna says it's because their parents don't want any of the kids going anywhere alone nowadays.

We hand out sheets to all the participants with all the sign language we're going to teach them. Then Tato springs the surprise: "You will decide what other words to teach the dolphins this week. You can add a verb or another noun, but you'll decide as a group what it's going to be, and then we'll all work on teaching the dolphins this new word, and then build it into the sentences."

The kids are excited. Especially when they learn that everyone will be taking part in Colin's week-long birthday program. They will have various roles: either selling tickets, giving tours of the facility, leading demonstrations, or, for a select few, taking part as trainers in the shows. Everyone's clapping, except me. I can't shake the dark shadow looming over me. I still don't have a solution. I still don't know how to stop time.

First, we're in the conference room, practicing the sign language. This is the first step, and when we see that everyone's getting the hang of it, it's time to head out on separate tours. My group gets to meet the dolphins first. Cedric, Petro, and Anna are taking the other three groups to different areas of the facility for their tours. Eventually, one group and one dolphin will begin working with the communication building blocks. The rest are getting to know how we run the dolphinarium and are spread out everywhere from the reception and ticket office to the technical rooms and the kitchen.

The kids in my group are all chattering and beaming. I realize that Larissa is in my group, and when we enter the lagoon, everyone rushes to the pool.

I wave them all away. "Step away! You don't go to the pool until I say so!" I shout.

"You're being a bit bossy," Larissa says as she turns to me. She's not unkind about it. It's a gentle reprimand.

I swallow. I know she's right, but I can't help it. "I see you managed to get a spot," I say.

She shrugs. "I thought you could all use the support." She looks around as another group passes by with Cedric. "A lot of kids are interested in helping you guys, you know?"

I see everything in a new light all of a sudden. The eager faces. The love for the dolphins. The curiosity. Larissa nods at me, encouraging, then whips out her phone and slides over to me to take a selfie just as Roxi and Lily pop up behind us.

I'm not smiling like they are, but I'm also not defensive anymore. I turn to the group and get started.

"These are my girls," I begin. "This is Lily, and this is Roxi. They're our teenaged dolphins. Their moms were sent to Romania a couple of years ago." I pause and look at Tato, who's getting the experimental pool ready in the adjacent room. Is that when our financial troubles appeared? Was that why we sold the mamas?

"Now, here comes Colin," I say, and drop down to the rim. Colin rises up and kisses my cheek. The kids all *ooh* and *aah*, and I suddenly get a knot in my throat. These are my last moments, and I feel like we're all too late. The interest in our dolphinarium, the sea mammals, our work . . . Why didn't we do all of this earlier?

The kids are waiting for something to happen, so I talk about Colin's age spots, and how to tell the difference between the dolphins. When Pesyk barks and growls, they all laugh. I then tell them how, when I was three years old, I began riding Fizz. I look at him, curious. He escaped the Soviets before, as a military marine mammal, and I'm about to tell the group this, but then I stop. He *escaped*.

"Sofiya," Tato calls in that official tone. "It's time to channel Colin into the experimental pool.

I bend down and look at Fizz one more time; the kids are still clamoring over the whale. One at a time, I herd them toward the experimental pool, where my group is allowed to get up close and personal with Colin. We play ball with him and hand out ice cubes, and I just let the kids get to know him.

"How are you doing?" Tato asks me.

"Fine, I guess."

"You don't look fine. Aren't you excited?"

I toss a hoop into the pool and turn to Tato. "I'm excited. But I'm also really sad."

He scratches his beard and squeezes my shoulder. "I know."

"What are we going to do?" I whine to him. Larissa is taking one selfie after another with each of the other members of my group.

Tato winks at me, but his eyes are dark. "One step at a time, Sofiya, okay? One step at a time."

I look around. "Where's Major Chaban?"

Tato raises his eyebrows, and his mouth flicks up into a

smile. "Happens to be that he and Ilya were scheduled for some sort of vacation this week and next. We've got the place to ourselves in the meantime. Let's enjoy it as long as we can."

As long as we can . . . Before I can think much further about it, the door opens and Pesyk's group arrives to work with him. Petro is leading that one. Pesyk pops his head up in the lagoon and growls and barks. Again, all the kids are laughing, some nervously, but I laugh because I love him so much. I love them all, so much. I'd like nothing more than to just jump into the water—clothes and all—and give Pesyk a big hug.

So I abandon my group, rush back into the lagoon, and do exactly that.

By the end of the second week, the camps are a *huge* success! The kids came up with new commands and words, including *follow, boat, dive, do a headstand, flip, and circle around.* But I can't stop counting down the minutes, the seconds.

Tato wants to take us "leader" kids out to eat on the last camp day, and suggests a really nice restaurant, but all of us would prefer to go to Ivan Markovych's food truck. It's a beautiful afternoon, and Cedric, Petro, Anna, and I line up on the seawall with our warm tacos and sodas. Denys is also with us. Our feet are kicking the air freely, and the wind is a little chilly, but there is the promise of summer in the air. The trees are filling out: the willow over the food truck, the palm trees along the promenade, the lilac bushes. Everything is great. It's one of the few moments when I think maybe things *aren't* going to change.

But then I see Tato and Ivan hunched over together, not over a chess game as they usually are but standing with strong cups of coffee and gesturing. Ivan keeps flinging his arm out to the right. Tato rubs a hand over his head, and I see his chest expand. I look to where Ivan is pointing. And then I see it. A big billboard, reflecting in the setting sun. It has a smiling young boy and girl, about Denys's age, and a sign that says CRIMEA! WE ARE ALL ONE! And the colors of the Russian flag, of course.

"Hey, I have some news," Cedric says suddenly.

I turn my attention to him.

"I heard that some of the teachers are being told that if they don't apply for Russian passports, they won't have jobs anymore. They're doing it at the university."

"What?" Petro asks.

Anna and I repeat the question. "Why?" I add.

"Because that's how it works," Cedric says, as if we should know.

"Has Ilya said anything to you about the camps?" Anna suddenly asks.

"I haven't talked to him since the night Major Chaban came into the dolphinarium and took it over."

"He betrayed us," Petro says. "I don't care what he says or does, he is not to be trusted."

Denys lays his taco off to the side. "I heard someone talking in school, saying how he's an ethnic Russian. That's the whole argument for the Kremlin to be here. To protect the ethnic Russians." He points to himself, Petro, and Anna. "We're the enemy! Because we prefer to speak Ukrainian in my family. That's their whole rationale for this."

I look back at Ivan and my father. "Ivan Markovych said I will have to choose one day. That I'll have to choose what I am."

Denys has a soft mustache and a goatee, and looks older than he is. But he's really nice, so I'm surprised when he asks hotly, "What are you going to be, then, Sofiya? Ukrainian or Russian?"

"I'm neither. I'm half-half. My mother is Russian. Tato is Ukrainian. Babushka has roots in Crimea and is half Tatar, half Ukrainian. Do I really have to choose?"

My friends look at one another.

Denys nods slowly. "Yeah. You will really have to choose."

Cedric, who has some magic way of breaking tension when necessary, suddenly hands us his cell phone. "Look, our videos from the camp are going viral."

Anna moves over and peers over my shoulder, one arm around me, as if to make up for Denys's hard opinion. I watch the dolphins swimming about in the video. Fizz is with them, too.

"You know," I say to the phone, "I always think of the pod as just the four dolphins, but as far as Fizz and they are concerned, he is part of it. He's a part of the dolphinarium, the family. All of them are, and the sea lions. They are, too."

Petro takes the phone from me. "You know? We could have really used Ilya on those videos."

Everyone kind of makes a face, but Cedric is the first to nod.

I turn to Denys. "Colin was at the dolphinarium long before Lily, Pesyk, or Roxi arrived. I wonder if he felt that he was being invaded. I don't think so, though. If you look at the animals, they figure things out. That's what Babushka told me."

Denys looks off to the sea. "Like in a Disney movie?" He laughs a little. "It's a little naive . . ."

"When she was a girl, she brought her cat out to the dacha one summer and she was afraid that it would get eaten by a fox or a wolf. Her mother then told her that the animals figure things out amongst themselves. Then Babushka woke up one morning to see a baby deer playing with her big German shepherd. She told me that sometimes she believes animals can do better than humans."

I look over at Tato. He's pacing and Ivan is still gesticulating wildly, his voice raised. And now I hear some of his words.

"You . . . Russian passport . . . never forgiven! Nobody will understand! You'll be considered a traitor!"

Traitor? Tato bought us some time by working with Major Chaban. He's trying to do better. My mother could have done better. The Russians *have to* do better. But I don't know if they can. Can *we*? We're just kids . . . And my head is all mixed up. But then I remember my Easter dress, and what Babushka said, and what I know about us, about our family, and our history. We're *here*. My mother is in *Russia*. She went *back* to Russia and left us here.

"I'm Ukrainian," I say to all my friends. I turn to the billboard. "Crimea is Ukraine. Not Russia. I'm Ukrainian. And I'm going to be a *Ukrainian* marine biologist."

Denys leans back a little, his eyebrows raised. "Sounds like you've made your choice."

We all look out onto the sea, and finish our tacos. But I think we all know this is not the end of it.

CHAPTER 22

Fizz and the Sea Lions

On Easter morning, I wake up and all I can think about is that I still don't have a plan. And as far as Tato is concerned? He doesn't seem to have one either. Not even Babushka has words of wisdom right now, and they both actually forbid me to talk about the dolphins.

"It's a holy day," she says. "A day of celebrating new beginnings."

New beginnings? I want to scream!

Are we just going to keep on going without finding a solution for the pod? Are they all just going to accept what is happening and look for a *new* beginning?

Again, I think of that little boy Tato saved in the deflating tube on the sea, and wonder where is he now when *I* need him? When my *pod* needs him?

After a very quiet Easter lunch with Babushka, Tato asks me if I want to go to the dolphinarium with him. Of course I do. Every moment counts now.

We bike under partly cloudy skies. Along the way, I see that nearly every other tree trunk has a small yellow ribbon attached to it. Tato stops at one and reaches out to stroke it. It's got a single loop, like the pink breast cancer ribbons.

He looks around and scratches his beard. "Looks like some people are staging a revolt."

"What do you mean?"

He looks down at me and takes in that breath, then puts a hand on my shoulder. "Nothing."

But it isn't nothing, is it? Because my heart lurches at the thought of a revolt. We bike on, and I forget the ribbons because we're both surprised to see Major Chaban's Mercedes in the lot. He and Ilya must be back from their holiday trip. There's also a very large and unmarked semitruck parked outside, with the motor running. On a Sunday?

Tato inspects it. The driver is not there. The cab is locked. Russian plates. He taps on the back and then marches inside.

We're in the underground area and I point to the first glass. "Look, Tato! The sea pen. It's reopened."

"What the . . ." Tato mutters. "Are they planning to put the animals out into the open sea? They can't do that!"

He pushes through the PRIVATE! door that only staff are allowed to use, and we hurry upstairs and into the hallway. I hide behind Tato as he knocks on the office door—*his* office door—and opens it without waiting for an answer. Major

Chaban and Ilya are both there, Ilya leaning back in a chair and snapping gum.

Both of them straighten. Ilya's chair swings down with a big clatter.

"Why the sea pen?" Tato asks. "It's been proven that the animals get sick."

"We'll need them to train the dolphins with the navy."

"But this harbor is too polluted. The noise causes too much stress for the animals."

"If they can't handle it?" Major Chaban shrugs. "Survival of the fittest. We only care about the elites."

I'm stunned. Tato makes a growling sound.

But Major Chaban drops the pen in his hand onto his desk and closes a file. "I've just been calculating how much the camps brought us. It's not nearly as much as you say they did."

I hear motorized noises behind me, and I nudge Tato. He hears it, too.

"What's going on?" he asks, but he is already hurrying out into the hallway.

I follow him to the lagoon and the sea lions' pool. We both come to a screeching halt, like in the cartoons.

The sea lions are barking like mad, but their room is empty. Except for two crates. They are packed up in there. Just then, someone drives in with a forklift and picks up the pallet. My heart lurches. In the adjacent pool room, the first thing I see is a crane erected on the side of the basin and a hammock. I hear the squealing before I recognize that it's Fizz's melon and rostrum poking out!

"What are you doing?" I shout.

Tato rushes over in his shoes and socks and gets straight into the water. "You can't do it like that! You have to watch out for his fins!"

I am struck dumb. He's going to *help* them pack up Fizz? And take him where?

I spin around and Ilya is there, his eyes are wide and stuck on me.

"They're off to the Arctic," Major Chaban says as he strides in. "The whale and the sea lions."

"What?" I scream. "How? Why?"

Tato wades back out, dripping wet; he's fuming in front of Ilya's father. Ilya shrinks back against the wall and spits out his gum into his hand.

"You said we had time. Until May!" Tato shouts.

"The dolphins are staying. But our military is taking the three other animals to integrate into their Arctic program."

Tato growls. "We'll see about that!"

He jumps back into the water as the crane lifts Fizz into the air. Fizz's head is thrashing about in the hammock, his mouth is open, and he's blowing hysterical noises through his blowhole. I look wildly back at where the forklift is driving down the ramp with the seals. First, Fizz. I jump into the water, too, just before he's out of reach.

"Fizz! Fizz!"

Tato shouts for the soldiers to stop the crane. "For heaven's sake! Let her say goodbye to him, would you? She's been riding that whale since she was three!"

I can't say anything other than his name as I stroke his melon. I'm crying so hard. Finally, I get it out. "Goodbye, Fizz. Goodbye. Don't forget me. Please, don't forget me. I love you!"

Tato has to pry me away. He leads me out of the water, and someone—Tetyana, I think, I don't know because I can't see anything through my tears—hands me a thick towel.

Hands on his hips, Tato faces off against Major Chaban again, and his voice cracks when he asks, "And then what, Ilya Mikhailovich? *Then* what?"

"Then you're done," Major Chaban says. He turns as the crane lowers Fizz into the transport crate. "Unless you get yourself a Russian passport." Now he looks back at my tato and his mouth flicks up. "And sign up for the military. That goes for all of your people. And that's to be done before that ridiculous dolphin birthday show. Otherwise, you will see that we will put on an entirely different show for the public. I don't believe it will take long for Colin to remember his training from the Soviet days."

I stare at them all. I can't believe it. Tato is backing away from him. He throws his hands up in the air and rubs it over his head. He's stammering. He prowls the rim of the pool and yanks at his bun.

"I don't know, Ilya." Tato's talking to Major Chaban, but Ilya Ilyich steps away from the wall. He turns and leaves the room.

"Go!" I scream at him. "Just go! All of you, just go and leave us alone!"

I run out, out of the dolphinarium, and out into the street. In the park, I see that someone has painted all the park benches blue and yellow, the colors of the Ukrainian flag.

I stop and throw myself on a bench. I can't stop the tears, though. I need a new plan. Not a new beginning, a new *plan*! I need help. We need the whole world to protest this. And now even Tato has given up. How could he have let them do this? He even *helped* them put Fizz in that crate. There is only one person left who might be able to help: Miss Yvette.

CHAPTER 23

Banished

Miss Yvette is the only reason I can even pull myself out of bed and go to school the next day. Talking to her, formulating a plan, is my last drop of hope in getting Fizz and the sea lions back. In finding a way to save my pod. But when I pull into the schoolyard, Cedric appears from around the corner. Immediately, I can see that something is very wrong.

I hurry over to him and throw an arm around his shoulders. I don't even ask. I'm not sure if I can bear any more bad news.

Cedric swallows, and his eyes are on the ground. He shrugs under his yellow windbreaker.

"My dad . . . My dad told me we're moving back to Nigeria. After the school year."

"You can't," I say. But it's a mere whisper. I shake him a little. "You can't leave me."

Anna and Petro show up moments later where Cedric and I are sitting on the stoop, ignoring Ilya and the Idiots, who are lounging on the opposite side of the entrance where they always seem to keep guard, waiting to pounce on a new victim.

Cedric and I tell the twins the news, and they slump down

next to us, Anna's bag clunking onto the concrete step below her.

"Two months," Cedric says. Then he looks at me. "But at least I'll be here for Colin's birthday show."

I moan and drop my face into my hands. The tears again.

"Hey? Hey," Petro repeats. "What's that about?"

I raise my head and swipe my face. I take a deep breath and tell them about Major Chaban sending Fizz and the sea lions to the Arctic. "For experiments. For training. What do I know? But he said the costs were too high to keep all of the animals."

"And the pod?" Anna asks. Her eyes are flashing beneath her dark bangs.

I shrug. "I need a plan. I wanted to talk to Miss Yvette about it."

Anna looks up at the building where the clock is ticking. "Then let's go. Now. Before the rest of the class gets there."

We jump up and I take a moment to appreciate my friends. I throw my arm over Cedric's shoulders again. "Maybe the U.S. or the European Union will help. Maybe there's hope. Until then, Miss Yvette might have some ideas . . ."

We all come to a standstill outside English class. There is a large woman with a mane of dark blond hair on her head, wearing hot pink lipstick and a gray Argyle-pattern vest over her blouse. She's older than Tato but not as old as Babushka. Somewhere in the middle.

She stands up and starts speaking Russian to us. "Are you in English first period? Come, take your seats. What are your names?"

"Who are you?" Anna asks bluntly.

The woman looks taken aback; she brushes her arms down her wide sides and folds her hands in front of her. "I'm Mrs. Vitalia Gonorova."

"Where's Miss Yvette?" Anna demands.

"Yeah," I say. "Where's Miss Yvette?"

"Miss . . . *Yvette* will not be back. She has left the peninsula."

I clamp a hand over my mouth again. "No . . . No!" I say into it. I turn to Petro. "That's not possible. She didn't even say goodbye?"

The woman sways a little in front of us, then turns sharply to her desk and pulls open a drawer. "That's not quite right. The director was going to give her the opportunity to say goodbye to you all, but she left notes for each of you instead. Your name?"

A *note*?

"Anna Polia," Anna says hopefully. "I'm Anna Polia, and this is my brother Petro."

"I'm Cedric Abara," Cedric calls.

They go up there and this woman—this Russian . . . I don't

know what to call her—tells my friends their individual "messages" from Miss Yvette.

Then the woman looks sternly at me. "And you? Do you want yours?"

"She's Sofiya Oleksandrivna," Anna says. "Of course she wants her message."

"Ah!" the woman says, like she's been waiting for this moment. "Miss Yvette writes here that you are exceptionally talented, a scientific and artistic mind. Someone right in the middle of it all in more ways than one. Here, she writes, 'Sofiya, do not waste any of it. Make sense of the world, but embrace the chaos, too. You can't control everything; sometimes to get what you need, you have to let go.'"

"Well . . ." The woman's eyes shift over me. "That's very philosophical. I don't know what it's supposed to mean, but you can at least control the grade you'll get in this class now. Go on, children. Take your seats."

I move to my seat as if I'm underwater. But not in a good way. I mull over Miss Yvette's note. *Let go? Let go of what?*

I'm in the Land of the Lost. The Land of the Banished. I'm losing everything again: Fizz, the sea lions, Miss Yvette, I'll be losing Cedric, and even my Ukrainian passport if Mr. Chaban has his way. I'm not in control of a single thing right now. Nothing at all!

"Who is going to help us now?" I ask nobody in particular.

All of a sudden, we hear mean-sounding laughter down the hall, and then I see him. The root of all my problems: Ilya Ilyich.

Before I can think about it, I push myself out of my seat and charge into the hallway. I don't register Mrs. Gonorova's calls. I hear them, but they mean nothing to me.

I'm the shark this time. And I'm on the attack.

Everything around me fades as I target Ilya Ilyich.

My heart pounds in my ears.

The impact takes my breath away. The next thing I know, Ilya is under me and I scramble onto my knees, and I feel a sharp pain. But I just start pummeling. Anything I can find. I hardly land a couple of punches when I'm ripped off him. His arms are covering his head. His backpack is askew on the ground. My ears are roaring, like I'm too deep underwater, but not the way it is when I'm in the dolphinarium. Everything is just . . . slow motion. Heavy. And red. I see red.

Ilya slowly gets to his feet, and I see the hot pink lipstick of Mrs. Gonorova in my face. She is spitting mad. She whips me away and marches me down the hallway to Director Vovk's office. I just go. I don't even fight it. If this is what Miss Yvette meant about letting go, then she is just wrong. Just all wrong.

Mr. Vovk's pointy eyebrows are raised warily at me. He taps the dark wooden desk with his fingers. It is just him and me this time. Somehow, Ilya was spared.

"Here we are again," he says in Ukrainian.

I look up from my lap, surprised. He was the one who told us the language is forbidden.

He leans in. "Sofiya Oleksandrivna, what is it that is bothering you? What is it between you and Ilya Ilyich?"

"Besides the fact that he's a rashist?"

Mr. Vovk blows out of his mouth, then wipes his whole face. "It's not going to get any better, is it?" he asks, still in Ukrainian.

I fold my arms and lean back. Vovk is a Ukrainian name. Maybe he'll understand?

"I'm losing everyone," I start slowly, and have to blink away the sting in my eyes. I don't want to cry in front of him, but my voice cracks. "I lost my mother. Cedric's family will return to Africa. I'm losing the dolphins. Fizz is already gone. The sea lions . . . Even Ivan Markovych said he'd go out east and fight the insurgents if he has to. Russia is ruining my life."

"Ivan who?" Mr. Vovk asks.

I swipe at my face and sniff. My bottom lip is trembling.

Mr. Vovk rests his elbows on the desk. "Never mind. He's obviously someone important to you. All right, Sofiya. I hear you. But what is your plan? To fight everyone?"

"Why did Miss Yvette leave?" I ask, and the stupid tears escape again.

"Oh . . . that. Well . . . there was nothing we could do about that, Sofiya."

"Why not?"

"Because she did not want to leave, but the Russian school board did not give her a choice. They told her she was provoking her students. And she was—"

"Provoking *what*?" I argue. "That we learn to work together? That we see through the Russian propaganda spun on our television sets, on our radios, and now in our schools? Nothing makes sense anymore! Nothing!"

"I think, Sofiya . . ." Director Vovk reaches over and hands me a tissue. I take it, even if it's embarrassing to be crying like this in front of him. "I think you need to learn to accept that people can only decide—in the end—what's best for *them*. Miss Yvette is going to pick her fights carefully. She knew she was beaten. She knew to let go. But letting go of one thing doesn't mean giving up on everything."

I look up at him and narrow my eyes. "Is that what you told her to tell me? To make me learn to let go? Well, both of you are wrong. My tato, too. I'm going to fight! I'm going to fight for my dolphins! And I'm going to fight for the Ukrainians here!"

"Nobody ever said anything about not fighting, Sofiya. I think the letting go is about forgiveness. Of maybe just accepting and stop blaming everyone else for your disappointments."

I stare at him.

"Forgive Miss Yvette. She truly had no choice. Well, she did, but it would mean a jail cell for her."

"She won't even respond to my texts," I say. "I tried to get ahold of her. She might have been able to help."

"Her phone was confiscated," Mr. Vovk says.

I stare at him in shock. Just like Denys. I start to shiver uncontrollably. Now I'm frightened for Miss Yvette.

"Has she been sent to the special department?"

He frowns. "Special . . . No. No, I don't know anything about that. But she was escorted over the border."

What had Miss Yvette done?

"You never know," Mr. Vovk interrupts my thoughts. "There's the saying that people always meet twice. Maybe she's helping you by not being here right now. All I know is that people rarely leave those they love by choice."

He looks at the door. Nobody is there. In a whisper, he adds, "I spoke with your father. If anyone was at fault about what happened to Ilya's mother, it was Major Chaban himself who should own up to his role in the accident. This is not your fault either. We're all just trying to do the best that we can in a very terrible situation."

I look at Mr. Vovk. His brows are knitted together—two sharp bluffs across his forehead. And I think, *Who else do I need to forgive?*

Tato, for one. And Ilya Ilyich, I guess.

CHAPTER 24

Coming Home

I go through the back door of the house and into the kitchen quietly, hoping that nobody is home. But then I hear Tato's voice coming out of his bedroom, where he also has his very messy home office.

It's been a horrible day. I don't want to talk. I don't even want to have to think. So I pick up Neptune, take my wool blanket, and hide underneath it. I pull my knees up and make myself into a ball. Neptune's not having it, though, and he flees. I'm alone again. I guess I'll have to start getting used to it.

I hear Tato's voice coming nearer. He's in the hallway, and I scrunch myself into a small ball beneath the blanket.

"Is that so?" Tato says. At first I think he's talking to me, but he pads right past the living room and into the kitchen. I hear him yank the refrigerator door open. "That's really interesting. Kharkiv offered the same thing. Yes, all four dolphins. At least for the interim until the international community can decide where to place them. Yes, that's fantastic. Me? Well, I . . . Uh-huh. Uh-huh."

I lift my head from my pillow. Am I hearing this correctly?

I hear something liquid slopping into a glass. The screw top back on. I don't move.

"All right, well, I'll think about it. Odesa? Yes. Yes, I could imagine it. Yes. Yes. I'll tell her. She'll be glad to hear from Miss Yvette."

I tear off the blanket and sit up; my hair is in my face and frizzing out with static electricity. Tato's back is to me as he pushes the cordless receiver button and puts the almond milk back into the fridge.

Back under the blanket I go. He pads by again, but then I hear him stop.

"Sofiya? Is that you?"

Slowly, I lower the edge of the blanket. "Hi, Tato."

He drinks from his milk, just looking at me, then raises one eyebrow. "Did you hear everything?"

"Only part of it."

"That was Odesa. The dolphinarium there is making a bid to take all four dolphins."

I sit up and put the blanket off to the side.

"The whole pod? To Odesa? That's so . . . far away."

Neptune, eyeing the blanket, jumps up, and this time he marches into my lap and kneads my thighs.

"It's an option," Tato says softly. "Either way, you're going to have to get used to the idea that things are different."

That again! Letting go! I hate everyone right now! Then I remember what he said on the phone. "And what about Miss Yvette?"

"Oh, you heard *that* part. Apparently, she's in Odesa, too, and she's getting a petition started. In your honor. She's trying to take it to parliament in Kyiv and get the government involved in negotiating for the dolphins."

Tears spring to my eyes. "But what if it doesn't work? What if the petition doesn't go through in time?"

"Well, that is the dilemma, isn't it? There is a home for our pod in Odesa, where they can live safely. The difficulty now is figuring out how to get them there before it's too late. But we will do everything in our power. All of us."

I leap up and fling my arms around Tato's waist. How could I have ever doubted him? *Either* of them. "I'm so sorry, Tato. I'm so sorry. I've blamed you for things that you are not responsible for. I'm no better than Major Chaban blaming Mama for Ilya's mother's accident."

"That's not true, Sofiya." Tato tips my chin up so I have to look him in the eye. "You've got a temperament, that's true, but I know you are grieving."

I swallow a sob and nod against his chest. "Cedric and his family are moving back to Nigeria at the end of the school year."

Tato lets go of me and runs a hand over his head. "I'm so sorry, Sofiya. That's got to hurt."

I mutter, "And I got into a fight with Ilya Ilyich again."

"Uh-huh. Director Vovk called me already. I told him to cut you some slack. It's been a rough couple of months. He agreed, and said he informed your teachers that you left ill."

I pull back.

"What about you and Ilya? Did you apologize to him?"

I shake my head.

"Don't you think you should?"

I'm worried about something else. "Tato? If it doesn't work . . . If Odesa can't get the dolphins . . . Will you get a Russian passport?"

He sighs and leans against the wall, the one with the "hole" in it.

"You said you would do anything to protect them."

"If I do *that*, Sofiya, they could send me out east. Fighting has broken out in Luhansk and Donetsk. I'd be sent by the Russian army to fight Ukrainians! I can't . . . I can't do that."

I remember what Ivan Markovych was saying about traitors when we were at the food truck, when I was sitting with the kids on the seawall. There's nothing to say. I don't want my dad to go fight in a war . . . to be called a traitor by his own countrymen.

Tato stands up straight. "How about bean burgers and guacamole, to get up your strength, and when this is all over, I'll take you to the dolphinarium. I think you might find Ilya there."

I look up at him, surprised, but all Tato does is wink. "You're not the only one concerned about Colin."

And just then my phone pings. It's a notification from Ilya. A picture of him holding his forelock back with one hand and taking a selfie. I gasp at his face.

You gave me a black eye! I'll never live this down!

That evening, Tato drives us to the dolphinarium.

I get out. There are a lot of military trucks here. But before I can even approach the building, Ilya suddenly shows up on his American-style BMX bicycle. He skids to a stop, watching me with his one good eye.

"Can I talk to you?" I ask as he leans his bike against the wall.

He shrugs.

"Play nice." Tato winks at me. He says hello to Ilya, grunts at the sight of his black eye, and goes inside.

I wait until the door shuts. I've had too much time to think. "Did you know about Fizz and the sea lions? Did you know your father would send them to the Arctic?"

Ilya scuffs the ground with his shoe, his lock of hair falling over his eyes as he looks down. “No. And I thought your dad brought you here to say you’re sorry.”

“I’m not so sure I am,” I snap.

He flips his hair out of his face and glares at me with his good eye.

I put my hands on my hips. “Why did you give me access to the cameras? So that I can see what happens at the dolphinarium? But you never told your father?”

“Because,” he says, “it felt like the only thing I could do to help. You might be able to say no to your dad, to talk to him. But I can’t talk to mine. Not when his mind is made up. But I thought if I gave you something to use against him . . . I thought if you could see how the animals were being treated and then share those videos with the world . . . maybe it would pressure the Kremlin or the Russian military to put a stop to it.”

I open my mouth. I know this is what he was trying to tell me the night Major Chaban took over the dolphinarium, but I wasn’t ready to listen. “But if I expose them, they’ll just take down the cameras.”

“That’s true,” Ilya says.

“I don’t know what to do.”

“I don’t either. But is this your way of apologizing?”

“I was so angry with you,” I say through clenched teeth. “You lied to me. To all of us.”

Ilya suddenly looks at me with anger in his eyes. "So what? So what if I lied? You've got *everything*, Sofiya. A dad who cares about you! A cool hobby, here, at the dolphinarium. Great grades. Teacher's pet. What have I got? Nothing!" He whips his backpack off and throws it onto the ground. "I've got a father who is always disappointed because I'm not the one who died!"

He slides along the wall and lands on the ground, hidden behind his raised knees.

I don't know what to say. Is he crying? I quietly walk over to him and sit down next to him. His forehead is pressed up against his knees, and I can't see his face.

"Ilya, you're not the only one who lost a mother," I say. "Yours died in a freak accident. But mine? She just left me. She just . . . I don't know. My love for her was not enough to make her stay. My love . . . My tato's love . . . What is worse?"

Ilya raises his head and his face is all red, but there are no tears. "How can you even say that?" His voice is a hoarse whisper. His fists are balled up and when he speaks, his voice is really tight. "I don't care what happened to your mother. Why she left you. I don't care. You hear me? I'm not going to feel sorry for you. How dare you ask which is worse?"

I stand up. He's right. It is not fair to compare. He is absolutely right.

“I’m sorry,” I say. I stick out my hand. “I’m really, really sorry. Truce?”

Ilya takes it right away and I help him up.

Our hands pull apart and he wraps an arm around himself. “I should have told you what my father was planning. But you guys were all so excited. So . . . I just wanted to . . . I just wanted to belong. You know? Be a part of something important.”

My heart cracks. “Ilya, all this time I’ve been thinking about how much I want to go and find my mama. It’s what I needed the money for. For a bus ticket to Moscow. But now . . . ? Now all I want is to save my dolphins.”

He looks down at his feet. “Your dad has to say he’ll get a Russian passport.”

I shake my head. “He’s gone in there to say he won’t. He didn’t tell me that directly, but I know that’s why we’re here. There’s a dolphinarium in Odesa that’s offered to take them. It’s our only hope.” I tell him about Miss Yvette. About the petition. “But we don’t have much time. And if parliament doesn’t decide to negotiate for the pod, there’s no way to get them to Odesa.”

“Miss Yvette once told us we have to depend on ourselves, to organize ourselves,” Ilya says.

I gasp. Did 6C have the same lesson as we did? She

talked to them all about the Maidan, too? About . . .

"Razom," I say quietly. "We work together."

Ilya seems to mull something over. "I think I know a way. But we're going to need your friends. And the participants from the camps. I think I can help."

I stare at him, skeptical. "For real?"

"Yeah. What if *we* delivered the dolphins to Odesa?"

CHAPTER 25

#OperationDolphinSquad

In the park a few days later, my friends are silent as Ilya and I go over the plan we'd worked out together. Anna and Petro sit on a wildly grafittied bench: *Russia, Ukraine, Russia, Ukraine* scratched over and over, and splattered with slurs and swear words. The twins' skeptical expressions look identical. Cedric is chewing his bottom lip. I know what they're thinking. *How can we possibly trust Ilya?* Or, rather, they're questioning the both of us.

Ilya paces back and forth in front of an old Soviet monument. He keeps throwing me pleading looks. I'm the only one on his side right now.

Finally, Anna speaks. "You call this a plan?" she huffs. "Sabotage? Sneaking a boat into the harbor and freeing the dolphins into the wild?"

"She didn't say into the wild." Cedric wags a finger. "She and Ilya said into the hands of the activists and the people from the Odesa dolphinarium."

"Yeah," Ilya says, and looks at me for support. "Because releasing the dolphins into the wild would be like taking

Cedric's dog, driving him up into the mountains, and abandoning him there."

Cedric stares at him, bug-eyed. "You know I have a dog?"

Ilya darts a look to me. "Yeah. I know you have a dog."

Anna shifts on the bench. "How do you know the dolphins will go to the activists?"

"Because we've trained them to. *Follow boat*. That's the command, and someone on the other side will repeat it, because they know it." Now it's me who bites my lip. Maybe the plan *is* too wild.

Petro interrupts. "Who? How? Who will be waiting on the other side? And how do they know to be there?"

Ilya and I glance at each other like two conspirators, which we are.

"Tell them," he says.

Cedric takes a step forward. The twins lean toward me.

"I kind of snuck onto my dad's computer last night and opened a new email account and wrote to his contacts with that new account . . . like I was him—"

"You *what*?" Cedric's arms flop. "Sofiya Oleksandrivna Len!"

"I sent an email to the Odesa dolphinarium, letting them know that we, well, my tato, I mean, have arranged transportation for the pod on the day of Colin's birthday show, and that they should get ready for their arrival.

"And I sent Miss Yvette the sign language cheat sheet."

Petro gapes before he splutters, "You did *what*?"

"Is she going to help?" Cedric asks.

"She said she would write me back," I say. "I mean, she'll write to my tato . . ."

"And did she?" Anna demands.

"Not yet."

Ilya scuffs his shoe. "Yeah, not yet."

Cedric yanks down his jacket over his hips and turns slowly to the sea. "And who's going to cut the nets so the dolphins can escape? How are you going to get the dolphins into the sea pen in the first place?"

"Yeah." Petro turns to Ilya. "How did you even convince your father to let Colin's birthday show happen?"

I slowly raise my hand and wait until he sees me before I answer. "Major Chaban needs this show to happen for the money it'll bring in alone. Plus, like Ilya told him, it'll put him in a positive light. He's been trying to get the pod trained in the sea pen for their navy training." I pause and shake off the very idea of them becoming soldiers.

Ilya cuts in then. "He wants Colin to end the show by performing his routine as a military marine mammal in the sea pen. A transition from a civilian therapy and research dolphin into a soldier . . ."

I flinch again at the idea. But if things go right, Colin will never have to see that fate.

"And that's when I'll cut the nets," I say. "Anna, I need you to take my place in the pool. If my dad asks where I am, you all have to tell him that I'm sick. You need to convince him that I'll be back soon."

Anna points to herself. *"Me?"*

"In the meantime, Sofiya will get into her scuba gear and be in the sea pen to wait for the dolphins," Ilya explains, as if it's the most obvious thing in the world.

Anna and Petro both take deep breaths and sit back against the bench. Cedric raises his eyebrows and checks in with the twins.

Petro pushes his glasses up to the bridge of his nose and stares off into the distance. "A lot has to happen before we can go through with this. And we've only got a week."

Grinning, I reach into my backpack and withdraw my observation journal. "I've got it all planned out here."

Pages and pages are filled with details I've worked out with Ilya. I flip to the first page headed #OperationDolphin Squad.

"A lot of these are Ilya's ideas," I say.

Everyone looks over at him, and his cheeks turn pink. "I watch a lot of military spy movies . . ." he says.

"But this *isn't* a movie," Anna reminds him. "Sofiya, don't you remember what happened to our brother? To Denys?"

"And you need a *boat*," Cedric says in a really low voice. "Who has a boat?"

I look over at Ilya.

"I do," he says. "I mean, my father does."

Petro takes off his glasses and clears his throat. "You're going to steal a *boat*?"

"Honestly," Ilya says, "it's more like borrowing."

"Bending the rules," I say. "Not breaking them."

Petro shakes his head. "We're *twelve*. You don't have a *license*."

"I've been driving that boat since I was eight," Ilya says off-handedly.

"Denys could drive it," I say.

Anna and Petro look at each other. "No," they say in unison.

I shrug, angry. "Then *we're* driving it. Me and Ilya."

Petro stands up. "It's illegal!"

Ilya expands his chest and strides over to him. "This whole annexation is *illegal*!"

"And that brings me to my next question," Petro shouts hoarsely. "Why now? Why should we trust you? Why are you trying to help us? You're Russian. I'm Ukrainian. I'm supposed to be your enemy! *Sofiya* is supposed to be your enemy! And I thought you were *for* this annexation!"

"My father is an ethnic Russian, but my mother was half Ukrainian. I'm just like Sofiya, here. I'm in the middle."

"Pickle in the middle," I mumble.

"And no matter what *side* you were born on," Ilya adds, "you can still decide when something feels wrong. This occupation is just wrong."

Anna and Petro look at each other. Cedric moves to me.

I look Cedric in the eye. "My tato has refused to get a Russian passport. He can't risk being sent to fight for the Russian army. After Colin's show, the dolphinarium will be shuttered to the public. My tato will be out of a job." Anna and Petro move closer to me. "This is our last chance."

Cedric takes a deep breath. "Show me your plans," he says, indicating the observation journal.

I'm about to open it up again, but suddenly my cell phone pings. Then again. And again. My phone is blowing up with notifications as I grab it out of my coat pocket.

"It's Miss Yvette's Telegram channel," I call excitedly. "Look!"

Everyone gathers around me and I push the arrow to play the video. Miss Yvette's using one of those sticks to film herself and the background. First, she waves at the camera.

"We're here today with scientists, researchers, dolphinarium staff, and activists in Odesa, begging for the Russian military to release the dolphins of Sevastopol: Colin, Pesyk, Roxi, and Lily!"

We all look at one another in shock.

"We've got a petition with over fourteen thousand signatures for their release into Ukrainian hands. But the Kremlin does not recognize Kyiv's authority. So now it's up to the locals and the international community to take action . . ."

Now we all look at one another soberly.

Miss Yvette continues. "Colin's thirtieth birthday is just around the corner and we're taking this protest out onto the water! Because after this weekend, no civilian will be able to check on the dolphins. No civilian will be allowed at the facilities. And the Russians are pressuring the staff to accept Russian passports if they want to stay on to take care of *their* animals!"

"Yeah! Yeah!" I shout and I'm jumping up and down. "See! See! We *have* to do something!"

"We're doing this together," Miss Yvette calls from the recorded video. She turns around, showing the growing crowd. "*Razom!* Together we can be successful!" Then her face appears again. "This is Operation Dolphin Squad reporting from Odesa!"

I look up and stick my phone back into my pocket. Everyone goes silent and still.

"We're going to have to tell her the truth," I say quietly.

Ilya shakes his head. "Nuh-uh."

"If we want her to help, she has to know everything," I argue.

Anna steps up and puts a hand on my back. "Sofiya's right."

Ilya frowns and looks appealingly at Cedric. But Cedric blows a raspberry.

"You're the one who says we've got to do what's right," he says to Ilya.

Ilya sighs. "All right."

"Together," I say solemnly.

"Razom," Petro repeats. I swear it's become his favorite Ukrainian word.

We huddle up, like they do in American sports teams. Cedric's hand lands on top of mine. Petro is next. Then Anna. And last, Ilya. I look them all in the eye, and I see first myself in their reflection: curly blond knots, an orange hoodie, olive-green eyes. Then I see them: my friends. They are all going to pull through. I know it. For Colin, Pesyk, Roxi, and Lily, we're going to go beyond bending the rules. We're going to break them and get our dolphins out of occupied Russia.

I grin, pump my hand up and down, and shout, "Operation Dolphin Squad, let's go!"

CHAPTER 26

Sabotage

To be able to do what I have to do, I need to get myself out of the show. I'll have to pretend I'm sick. Being original, Ilya is also going to pretend he is sick and won't come to the show so that he can bike down to the harbor and *borrow* his father's speedboat.

Cedric and the twins are in charge of all the kids who are taking part in doing everything—from selling tickets and popcorn to giving tours behind the scenes—as well as a select few who are involved in the shows.

Tato's plan is to have all four dolphins in the waiting pool just off the sea pen. Which is what we need. Because the gate between the sea pen and the waiting pool is the only way the dolphins are going to be able to get out and follow me to their escape.

It's early Saturday morning on the day of Colin's birthday show. Today is the day. When I roll into the back lot of the dolphinarium, I spot our little orange Lada. Tato has been up extra early. But there is no Mercedes. Major Chaban isn't here yet. To my relief, there are only two military trucks—Major

Chaban's usual guards and the one trainer he has assigned from the navy to do Colin's military part of the show.

It's a warm, sunny day. The water is a dark, berry blue in the morning sun. But is it possible for darkness to fall just like that? Because when I go inside the dolphinarium, I realize that there is less and less light, although the days have been longer and sunnier. Every time I visit the dolphinarium, it's as if I've just put on a pair of dark sunglasses indoors. All the light is filtered out. Is that what happens when the people and animals you love go missing? Fizz and the sea lions have left another big hole in my life. And that hole will break completely open if this day doesn't go according to plan. If I have to let go of my pod. Of Colin.

I'm startled by the guard in the underground. A Russian soldier, but he's not carrying a rifle this time.

"Who are you?" he says.

"Sofiya Oleksandrivna Len. I'm the director's . . . Oleksandr's daughter. The head trainer? I'm supposed to meet him here. To prepare for the opening."

Ilya and I have been spending days together, remotely, watching spy movies and making more plans. We have all of our players: Cedric, Anna, and Petro are our decoys.

The guard motions for me to go on.

As soon as I am out the door, I veer right and slip out the

key for the basement, which I took out of Tato's spare set. I open the door. There is no floor, just a metal grate that gets me to the stairwell, where I will descend thirty-six feet down into the darkness. If it were my first time, it would be scary. But I've been down here a number of times. It's like going caving, and as I head down, the chemical smells hit me.

This is the belly of the beast, where all the water systems are channeled through enormous pipes that snake along the concrete floor. This is where all the magic happens to make this place run—where the salt is stored, where the technology is located for keeping the pools and lagoons clean, temperate, and pH balanced. As I pass beneath the smaller pipes, I have to duck under salt-encrusted stalactites. We keep calling for the technicians to come clean these up; even some of the gauges are coated in crystallized salt. Cedric once said it looked like battery acid, and poisonous. I thought so, too, but Tato told us it's not.

I pass by the research rooms and sick bay. If any of the animals get sick, this is where we put them. When Lily got injured, she was kept here for a little while. Otherwise, our animals have rarely needed to see the sick bay. My dad is a fanatic about keeping everything clean and proper. Which is why he is going to *freak out* when he finds out what I've done . . .

I've finally come to what I'm looking for. It's the system that keeps the pH levels measured. Tato figured out a way to install an alarm that's triggered in the case of a massive fluctuation in pH balance. If the alarm goes off, the gates of the pool then open, allowing the dolphins to be herded out into the sea pen until the levels are back to normal. That's where I'll be. Once they're in the sea pen, they'll be blocked off only by the nets at the edge of the harbor. And it's those nets that I will have to cut holes through.

I find the right pipes that lead to the staging pool. It's time for me to sabotage the pH balance. The dolphins will be halfway through their show when the alarms go off. With half a show left until the Russian navy trainer is scheduled to begin demonstrating Colin's special military talents. But I'm not going to let Major Chaban and his people get that far.

I watch on the U-Spy cameras as Tato puts together the staging area. I've seen one guard near the door in front of the sea pen. If I can just get him and Tato away from there, I can hide the scuba equipment I'll need to get into the water.

Just then, Anna and Petro hurry into the staging area, waving their arms. They're creating a false alarm and I see the guard straighten. They gesture to Tato, and he and the guard follow them out. I eventually see everyone appear on the monitor for the downstairs lagoon area. I don't have time to watch. I have to move. Now!

I slip into the staging area. The dolphins are gliding about peacefully, blowing and taking in air. I hurry out the door, my hands shaking. I am really queasy now as I hide the air tank, flippers, breathing apparatus, and mask among the rocks. Finally, I stash the metal cutters I borrowed from Tato's toolshed. I will need those to cut the nylon nets.

As I slide back inside and shut the door behind me, Colin glides past, one eye on me.

"This is it," I say shakily. "I'm going to help you. I need you to help me, okay?"

It's all I manage before I hear Tato's voice outside the auditorium. "Well, that was a waste of time, you two. But thanks for alerting us. Have you seen Sofiya? I thought she got here a while ago."

I have just reached the staging platform when Tato appears.

"There you are! Where have you been?"

I'm about to slide into the water, and Colin comes up and rests his rostrum on the rim.

"I'm ready to do the dress rehearsal," I say, avoiding the question.

"All right," he says. "Kids, take your positions."

When the soldier who is patrolling the area returns, I eye him, my teeth hurting because my jaw is so clenched. He has a bored look on his face as he takes up his position at the door again.

Anna and Petro come in, their eyes on me in conspiracy. Cedric winks a little, but I stop him and whisper, "Has anyone heard anything from Ilya yet?"

He was supposed to text me when he was on his way to the harbor.

"No word from him, no sign of his father," Cedric mutters just before my tato approaches. Cedric hands me my surfboard.

Rehearsal begins, but the Russian navy trainer insists on working with Colin alone. I stand on the rim, watching over my Colin as the trainer straps something weird to his beak and around his melon. Something that doesn't belong there.

"What is that?" I ask.

The trainer looks at me as if my question annoys him. "It's a spy monitor—a camera we can hook up to."

The idea of Colin wearing spy gear makes me want to throw up, but I pretend to be impressed so that the trainer will tell me more.

"And this on his beak helps to fight off enemy spies or trespassers," he continues. It looks like a spear.

"He attacks . . . ?" I stammer.

"Colin was trained to protect the harbor and the naval base. And, yes, to attack anyone who is not supposed to be there."

My Colin? *Attack?* I stare at my dolphin. "How?"

The trainer looks at Colin, impressed. "He can pull off a

diver's mask, for example, or flip off the breathing apparatus of a spy. Otherwise, he can grab them by the flipper and pull them up out of the water."

I look down at Colin. He's nodding in the water as if he wants to get the stuff off. But what the trainer says next almost knocks me over.

"Either way, Colin seems to remember his old training, too. Dolphins are the fastest swimmers. There is no technology that can replace them."

My jaw is clenched so tight now that I've given myself a piercing headache.

He can pull off a diver's mask.

Would Colin turn on me in the sea pen? Is it possible that he might not be able to recognize who I even am? Will he think I am the enemy if he sees me cutting the nets?

I walk over to Tato.

"I'm not feeling so well," I say. It's not a lie.

He touches my head. "Is it nerves?" Then he gives me that empathetic look. "I know this must be really hard."

I shrug.

"Babushka is coming in a little bit. She can check on you. Anna, can you help rally all the kids, get them into position? The doors will open in fifteen minutes."

Anna gives me a knowing look, then nods at my tato. "Major

Chaban just arrived. With a whole lot of other top brass."

That's the lingo she learned from her dad. It means a bunch of Russian military officers.

A shadow passes over Tato's face.

"Is Ilya with him?" I casually ask.

Anna's eyes flick to mine before they're back on Tato. She shakes her head.

All of a sudden, I realize I may not be able to pull this off. Tato's cell phone pings and he frowns at the screen.

"That's odd," he mutters.

"What is it?"

"There's a protest taking place just on the other side of the water. Miss Yvette . . . and the Odesa team."

He trails off and scratches his head. I try to still my heart. They're all there. It's happening.

Tato turns to me, concern crossing over his face. "You are looking pretty pale, Sofiya. Why don't you go lie down in the locker room for a while? We've got a little bit before the show yet. Maybe you'll feel better then."

"If not," Anna hurries, "I can take over for Sofiya."

Tato nods, distracted again.

Anna and I share a look, my heart thrumming in my chest, and I leave for the locker room.

A long time ago, Babushka told me about how she once

faked a fever as a child because she wanted to sneak away and visit the circus, which her parents couldn't afford. I rush into the locker room, turn on the hot dryers, and sit under them. I've been under them for a long time when I hear someone open the locker room.

"Kotyku? Sofiya?" It's Babushka.

I rush to the bench and lie down on my side, one hand hanging limply to the floor.

"There you are," Babushka says with concern. "What's wrong?"

I moan a little. "I'm not feeling very well."

She touches my forehead, frowns, and flips her hand and touches it again. "You're burning hot."

"My stomach is all queasy."

Babushka narrows her eyes and touches my face again. "Well, you certainly are not getting into that water. Should I take you home?"

I spring off the bench and run to the toilet, slamming the door behind me. I lean over, making gagging noises. I really do feel like I might throw up.

After a moment, Babushka knocks on the door. "Sofiya . . . I'll take you home when you come out."

"No, no," I call weakly. "Babushka, you really have to go watch the show. Please. If I can't get into the water, at least let me stay up here and watch from the monitors." I force out another fake gag. "I just want to be as close to them as possible while I still can."

Babushka sighs deeply. "All right, then," she says. "I'll let your tato know. But stay in the office and make sure to sip water."

I check my phone. Half an hour. I've got half an hour. And there is still no message from Ilya.

"Come on . . . come on . . ." I whisper. To Babushka, I call, "I'll be fine. Watch the show for me and I'll text you if I'm feeling any worse."

Babushka is giving me more instructions, but I'm too busy typing to listen.

Where ARE you? I text Ilya.

"Please keep your phone on you," Babushka says.

Finally, I hear her leave the locker room.

No answer from Ilya. Still no answer.

I look up at the clock.

I hear Tato's voice on the announcement board. "Everyone to the staging arena. We will begin our show in five minutes."

It's time for me to leave the building and creep out to the breakwater over the sea pen outside.

CHAPTER 27

Decoys and Diversions

While the crowd goes wild, my stomach sinks further and further.

No Ilya. Not a word.

I crouch behind the rocks outside in my scuba gear, watching the show on my app. Roxi and Lily are doing what they do best and stealing people's hearts. And we haven't even gotten to Colin yet. Major Chaban is flanked by a whole lot of top brass from the Russian military. Babushka is off on the sidelines. Once in a while, she throws a look toward the locker room, but I keep her concern at bay with an occasional text letting her know I'm just resting. Still, there's one problem.

I check Telegram. There it is—a whole line of boats with people dressed in blue and yellow. The Odesa staff are out there in white T-shirts with the dolphinarium logo on them. I catch sight of Miss Yvette in one speedboat. And then a *ping*!

It's Miss Yvette.

We're ready for you. All set?

I quickly type back. I'm about to write *I don't know where Ilya is*, but I quickly catch myself.

Our boat hasn't arrived yet. We're running out of time.

I watch as the three dots showing that Miss Yvette is texting appear and disappear.

Is there a trainer there able to swim with the dolphins? It's just over a kilometer to the border.

And then it hits me. How had I not thought of it before? Ilya *hates* swimming! Ilya *hates* the water! Why would he have ever offered to drive the boat himself?

I put my cell phone down. I've been so stupid. I trusted him. And all he did was get my hopes up, only to back out and abandon us.

I look toward the glass wall where I can see the show going on. Suddenly, Major Chaban stands up from his seat. He takes the microphone from my tato. I switch back to the U-Spy app and turn up the volume.

"Welcome, everyone! And now it's time to let you all know. We understand that there are great concerns for these wonderful animals here. But we've already got the Beluga whale, and the two sea lions you've likely seen here before, working in the Arctic, and doing wonderful things to help us explore our expansionist projects in the north. Russia is the greatest country on earth! Russia has the most powerful army and military! And these dolphins are going to be a part of that!"

There is polite applause except among that top military

brass. They're clapping with great enthusiasm.

And then it happens.

Peep-peep-peep!

The alarms. It's a sound like a smoke alarm.

Tato springs away from the stage toward the rim of the pool.

My heart is so far in my throat, I feel like I'm choking. But this is it. The gates is going to go up. I can see that the dolphins are swimming through to the waiting pool. Major Chaban is looking around in surprise. On the screen, I see his frown, and he's accusing Tato through the microphone. "What is going on here, Oleksandr? What is happening?"

And then there is another sound. The distant buzz of a motor, and from beyond the breakwater, I see it. A speedboat slowly inching its way around.

Ilya.

"Operation Dolphin Squad!" he shouts.

Every spy mission includes carefully placed decoys and diversions. The alarm is still going off as chaos breaks out in the arena. But I turn back to Ilya and I see everything clearly. Everything here is in order. I know what I have to do because I've drawn it all out. I drew a beautiful plan in the midst of madness.

I waste no more time. That sea pen gate is going to open up.

And that patrol is going to find me here if I don't get going.

I slip into the water. It's cold at first, and it takes me a few seconds to get my bearings in the murk. I can hear my heart beating. Schools of small fish dart about. Something makes a grinding sound. And there it is.

My dolphins are nosing their way out into the sea pen through the underwater metal door. I make for the nets, about fifty yards up.

I see Roxi. I see Pesyk. Lily glides past me as I near the nylon net. But where is Colin?

I don't have any time left. The adults are going to catch on to what is happening. Ahead, bobbing on the surface like a mirage on an oasis, is the bow of the motorboat. I can't believe Ilya came through.

I take out the cutters, and I begin. The hole has to be big enough that none of the dolphins can get tangled up. That means I have to make sure Colin can fit through it. I turn and look over my shoulder. The sea pen is a big area, and I see only one or two of the dolphins now, but the gate is still open.

When I give Ilya the signal, he'll whistle for their attention, and I will give them the commands they need to get out of here. But there's still no sign of Colin.

I cut. It's not easy. I have to press really hard. Nylon doesn't snap like metal does. It frays in spots, like when you're trying to cut fabric with a pair of paper scissors. Suddenly, the cutters slip in my hands and I nearly lose them.

My heart freezes. If they drop, it's deep. Too deep. I would have to dive down to get them. I can't afford the time to do that. What Ilya and I learned in all those movies is that the element of surprise lasts only a little while before someone—and in my case, it's going to be Tato, or Babushka, or Major Chaban, or the patrol just behind that door—is going to come to the conclusion that they've been had. And that us kids are behind it.

The next hole. The next one. I keep cutting and make sure I hang onto those cutters for dear life. The dolphins have caught on that I'm in the water with them. Now they're taking passes, clicking and whirring, sending creaking noises through the water. They're curious. I might not need Ilya at all to get their attention. They might just hang around me so that I can get them out. As if they know what I'm trying to do. As if they know the danger they're in if they stay here.

The hole is big enough for Pesyk, which means Lily and Roxi can fit through. Six more squares and I can make sure that Colin doesn't get tangled up. But where is he?

I turn again to see if I can find him. *What's this?* I scream into my breathing apparatus. Heading straight for me, at full speed, is Colin. In military gear.

And I am his target.

CHAPTER 28

Swimming with Spies

Without thinking, I drop the cutters.

The trainer from the Russian navy told me nothing that I didn't know before. There is no man-made technology that works better for echolocation than a dolphin's. There is no faster swimmer. There is no more intelligent sea mammal. Nothing more trainable. And like dogs, they retain *all* their training.

There's only one thing I can do. I push through the hole in the net and hope Colin can't reach me. The hole is still not large enough for Colin without getting him tangled up, but that's also what I'm worried about.

Colin swims toward the net, toward me, but veers to the right at the last second, that pointy canister on his beak like an extra robotic limb. The harness on him looks uncomfortable. My limbs are ice-cold as he charges and veers to the side again. I'm terrified now. If he tries to swim through the net and gets caught, it would be hard to untangle him by myself. But if I find a way to free him, I could be his target.

I look down at the seafloor. The cutters are there, gleaming in the wan light. I look up at the surface of the water. Behind me, the boat is inching closer. Ilya was supposed to remain hidden behind the breakwater. We can't let anyone know we're here trying to free the dolphins. Not yet.

There is no other decision to make. If I'm going to rescue the pod—with or without Colin's military gear on—I need those cutters.

I dive down. And suddenly, I see Colin through the net doing the same thing. He's slow. He's gliding. Not doing a cartwheel, but suspended upside down and swimming with me. I try to ignore him. I need that tool.

But when I reach the bottom and stretch my hand through the net to reach the cutters, I realize that it's too far away. If I'm going to get those cutters, I'm going to have to swim back through the hole to the other side of the net. Back into the pen with Colin.

I right myself up.

Colin rights himself up. He comes close. Really close. And he is calm.

I reach through the net. Underwater, everything slows down. Underwater, I remind myself, there is just nothing—absolutely nothing—that can go wrong. Colin turns so that he is sideways and really close to the net.

I do it. I touch him. I grab hold of the harness, and suddenly

I know all that I have to know. He's not going to hurt me. Never.

I figure out how to unclip the harness. Just then, a red light flicks atop the spy camera. Is it on? Panicked, I pull the mechanism off Colin's beak and let it drop to the seafloor. And then I signal with my hands.

Fetch cutters! I make cutting motions.

Colin peers at me, and then he's gone. He's swimming down, and then nosing up the cutters. He grabs them in his beak and swims back over to me. I take them. I have them. I kick upward and go back to my hole. One cut. Two cuts. Three cuts. Four. Clip! Clip!

The hole is big enough for Colin to swim through!

Fetch pod! I signal.

Colin disappears, but I hear the clicks and whirs nearing. Their higher-pitched sounds don't reach my ears. And then out of the gloom, four gray shapes are headed for me. I raise my hands—the signal I use for the entire pod to be still and wait for the next command. I swim to the net and pull up the top part.

Swim through! Wait! I command, and make a rolling motion with my arm for them to go.

Colin heads out first, spinning to the side. My heart is beating in my ears. Though I'm hovering over the hole in the net, I can swear his eye is on me. He trusts me to get him through.

I am suspended in the water, with this bird's-eye view of my pod. My family.

Click-click-click-click! Colin gently brushes by me as he passes through the hole in the net. The others are swimming in a slow circle below me, waiting for their turn. I look beyond the net to make sure Colin stays nearby. The rest are coming through now. First Lily. Then Roxi. Pesyk is last, all of them gliding beneath me and into the open sea. But they are staying close. I hold my finger up, and Colin comes near. He's waiting.

Fetch person! Swim boat! Pod follow!

It's three sentences. Three whole sentences for Colin. We've only ever managed two. Three has sometimes been too much. But his first response is to swim over to me so I can latch onto his dorsal fin. I hear him calling out and somehow I know he's understood it all. I know the pod is going to follow. One by one, Lily, Roxi, and Pesyk respond, their calls echoing like creaks on wooden stairs. Colin heads toward Ilya and the boat.

But just as we reach the end of the breakwater, and the full boat appears ahead of us, something disturbs the surface of the water. My eyes widen behind my mask.

A set of limbs is thrashing in the water in front of us.

Ilya!

I'm about to give the command *Fetch person!* but I can already feel Colin surge forward. I push myself forward, too, and I am nearly eye to eye with him for just a split second. Me and Colin. He doesn't need signals from me. He knows what we know.

All of a sudden, the other three dolphins pass by me. I slow down. Ilya's eyes are bulging, panicked, and I see the air bubbles escape from him, just before he gives up. His body folds in half—legs and arms raised toward the surface—and he slowly starts to sink.

I scream into my breathing apparatus. But the dolphins are already beneath him. I know what they're going to do. I kick myself to the surface and swim for the boat's edge. I duck back underwater to monitor what is happening. The dolphins are all carefully swimming around Ilya as Colin noses him up and to the surface.

I yank off my fins and my breathing apparatus, and drop the air tank into the boat. And then it comes. *Whoosh!* Colin's puff of air, and a hard gasp from Ilya.

"Ilya!" I cry. "Ilya!"

Ilya is spluttering at the surface, thrashing again.

"Grab hold of his dorsal fin! Grab hold! Colin will keep you up!"

Ilya is grasping blindly, and he finally latches on. Slowly,

Colin brings him closer to the boat. I yank him up, trying to get my balance before I fall in, too. Colin nudges him over to the ladder. As soon as Ilya has a hand on the rung, all four dolphins pop up, chattering away, as if they're all scolding him. I yank him over the rim of the boat.

Ilya braces himself against his thighs, gasping for breath.

"What on earth happened!" I cry.

Ilya, still taking deep breaths, only points behind him. "I . . ." he gasps. "Had. To. Warn. You."

I look to where he's pointing.

And that's when I hear the noise over the dolphins' chatter. The pod isn't scolding us. They're *warning* us. Along the shoreline of the sea pen, people are all lined up. Civilians. But my heart stops beating at the sight of military personnel charging over the breakwater.

Anna, Petro, and Cedric are at the very edge, gaping at us.

Babushka screams my name from the pier over the sea pen. She's got something in her hand, is waving it. With a gasp, I realize she's got my observation journal! I must have left it in the locker room! The whole plan is in those pages!

"We have to go!" I shout to Ilya. "Can you get this boat started?"

Ilya shakes himself off. I find a towel on the bench and throw it over his shoulders.

He goes to the motor and gets it started.

"Colin!" I frantically search for my whistle, but he pops back up as the other three dolphins circle the boat, gliding around us, waiting to follow.

"Run! Follow boat! Run!" I shout, signing the command at the same time.

Ilya looks back at me, his face grim.

"Go!" I say.

And the boat picks up speed. Colin is ahead of the pod, keeping up with ease. Four gray shapes, like silicon waves in the sea. Ahead of us, I can just make out the boats of protesters on the horizon, growing larger the closer we get. My heart soars. Ilya reaches for the dash of the boat and hands me his cell phone. It's set to the Telegram channel.

We're coming! I quickly type.

And then I look behind me and, once again, I feel sick. Looming just on the edge of the breakwater is a big gray-green boat.

A military patrol boat is coming straight for us.

Worse than that, I see Tato leaning against the banister on the deck, as if he's about to jump into the water after us. And next to him, arms behind his back and chest puffed out—blown up as big as he can get—is Major Chaban.

CHAPTER 29

The Great Escape

"Faster!" I scream. But Ilya's eyes are wide.

"What if I run over a dolphin?" he shouts over the noise.

"You can't!"

Ilya carefully pushes the throttle forward and the boat surges ahead. He manages to put only a small distance between us and the Russian patrol boat.

But then we see it. On the shoreline ahead, the sign that indicates we are entering neutral waters. The Ukrainian protesters and their parade of boats are more recognizable now, not just dots in the distance.

"Slow down!" I shout to Ilya.

He slowly pulls the throttle, and the boat slows down. Suddenly, from both sides, the shadows of two more Russian navy patrol boats loom over us.

"Colin!" I yank the whistle up from around my neck and blow. "Colin!" I shout again.

Colin comes up. So does Roxi.

"The other two are over here!" Ilya shouts.

I suddenly get tears in my eyes. This is goodbye. And we

don't have time. I don't have time to even touch them, to stroke them one more time.

"Sofiya!" Ilya suddenly screams. "They're going to close us in!"

And I suddenly see why. The two other patrol boats that have appeared on either side of the harbor have nets spanned out from the rear. They're dragging nets and creating a giant wall. They are trying to trap the pod behind the Russian border.

I know what I have to do.

I raise my finger, and I give the command. *Fetch pod! Swim through! Run! Follow boats!* I point to the protester boats in the distance. Colin and the pod are all on me, though. That's four sentences. *Four!* Can they do it? Can Colin lead the pod and follow all four and do them in that order? But what if he follows the patrol boats instead?

Colin chatters and whirs. He shovels water all over Ilya, soaking him again. Ilya lets out a laugh, but I see tears streaming down his face.

And then they are gone. Four gray dolphins slip away.

I don't breathe.

The patrol boats are only a few feet apart as the nets begin closing together.

"There!" Ilya shouts. He stops the engine before we crash into the Russian patrol boats.

I grab the binoculars off the dash and hold them up. I count as the dolphins break over the surface, through the teeny-tiny space left between those two Russian boats.

I count. "One! Two! Three!"

Just then, the two patrol boats intersect and the harbor is sealed off.

"I only saw three!" I cry. "Where's the fourth?"

Who got trapped? Which of my dolphins got left behind?

Through my tears, I see Ilya wipe his face. He grabs his cell phone and starts texting away at rapid speed. I turn around as a shadow falls over us. The Russian patrol boat approaches and I see my father's face. I see Ilya's father's face. They look nearly identical, but then Tato dashes away, climbing down the rope ladder, trying to get on board our boat.

"Look!" Ilya cries. He shows me the cell phone.

Miss Yvette is live on video.

"Operation Dolphin Squad! You did it! All four are here!"

A woman next to her blows her whistle. Miss Yvette turns the phone toward the water, and I see Colin's head pop up. And then I see three more heads pop up, all of them chattering and clicking and whirring. The staff are tossing them all fish. I laugh and cry into my hand at the sound of Pesyk's excited "barks."

The whole pod. My family.

Just then, the Odesa trainer raises a finger and gives the command *Follow boat!*

"Give me the key to the boat," I hear Tato call. I whirl around just as he jumps aboard.

I turn to him, but I'm so relieved, all I can do is slump onto the nearest bench.

"I did it, Tato. We did it."

His face is like a blank canvas as he snatches the key from Ilya.

Ilya sits down next to me. Suddenly, I feel his hand in mine. I look down. He's grasping it hard and staring up at his father, whose fire we can feel from the deck above.

Quietly and slowly, Ilya says, "We are . . . in *so* much . . . trouble."

CHAPTER 30

The Aftermath

"Are you kids okay?" Tato asks. Now in control of the boat, his face transforms into an expression of relief.

I nod. I can't talk. My heart is hammering so hard, I'm out of breath.

"Ilya?" he asks.

Ilya's hand slips out of mine. I look at the rope ladder where three Russian soldiers are ready to grab us.

Major Chaban is still glowering down at us. He puts a megaphone to his mouth. "Ilya Ilyich, get up here right now." Then he turns away and speaks really loudly, addressing the names of the two boats that drew the nets closed. "Retrieve those dolphins!"

But the patrol boats are still.

"Ilya Mikhailovich!" Tato shouts up. "They cannot invade neutral territory. It's enough! It is *enough*!"

Major Chaban turns and glowers down at him. He then jabs a finger at Ilya, who still hasn't moved from my side, and points to the waiting men in scarves that cover everything but the eyes.

I grab Tato's arm and yank it. I plead with him in silence. *He can stay here, can't he?*

Tato rubs a hand over his hair. His face is pale. "Ilya, I'm going to take over the boat, okay? If you want to stay with us, though . . ."

Ilya lowers his head and shakes it. "I have to go." He turns to me. "We did a good thing, Sofiya, didn't we? We did the *right* thing."

I still can't speak. I can only nod.

Major Chaban's voice booms over the water again. "Ilya, get in the boat."

But Ilya does not move.

"I'm your father. You *will* obey me."

Ilya deflates before my very eyes. Tato puts his hands on his shoulders and draws him close, but speaks to us both.

"You two have proven that, if you work together, you can get things done. You got things done, Ilya." He glances up at Major Chaban, then takes us both by the shoulders. "There will be a day when the two of you are old enough to make the decisions that influence a country. For now . . . you still have some growing up to do. And a lot to answer for. Part of growing up is taking responsibility for your actions."

I hang my head.

"Hey," Tato continues. "I'm proud of you. Both of you.

What you did . . . all of you, is nothing short of amazing. But if Sofiya hadn't left her observation journal in the locker room . . ."

I shiver. "Babushka found it?"

Tato tilts his head. "It's what she was reading before the show started. She realized what was happening as soon as the alarms went off."

Ilya and I look at each other sheepishly.

"We could've been too late," Tato warns. "And you two . . . You've broken so many laws. You *stole* dolphins."

My heart drops as I suddenly remember what happens to provocateurs. Tato and I will be on a list. And Ilya? I don't know if even Major Chaban has the power to get him out of this one.

But Tato is grinning at me, his eyes sparkling with mischief. "You *stole* dolphins!" Then his eyes crinkle, and I can tell he wants to laugh, but he coughs into his fist instead. "All right, Ilya. It's time to face the music."

Ilya cautiously moves to the rim of the boat. Tato helps him balance until those little green men—those Russian aliens—grab hold of him and help haul him up onto the deck.

Major Chaban lowers his binoculars and faces his son.

"They're gone, Ilya Mykhailovich," Tato shouts up at him. "Those dolphins are safe. But I will take your boat back to the harbor. If you're going to arrest anyone, it should be me."

"You better believe I will," Major Chaban shouts down at him.

"All right," Tato says. "If that's what you think is the right thing to do. But your son nearly drowned a second time in his life," Tato says loudly. "We all saw what those dolphins did. He is now standing here in front of you, alive and safe because of them."

Major Chaban's face ripples with something I've never seen before. Pain? Grief? And relief.

He suddenly strides over to Ilya. Even from where I stand, I can see he is shivering. I hold my breath. Is his father going to hit him? But when his arms come up, it's to take Ilya by the shoulders. He shakes him a little, his face still full of emotion. He then takes an emergency blanket and wraps it tightly around him. It's almost an embrace. Major Chaban steers Ilya away from us, and I watch the two disappear from sight.

Tato looks at me. "Are you okay?"

"Yes," I finally say. "Yeah. I'm okay. But . . . are you going to have to go to jail?" I think of that special department for provocateurs.

Tato takes me in his arms and wraps a fresh towel around me. He gently leads me to the bench and kisses the top of my head. He does as I do and avoids answering the question.

"Babushka is worried to death. Let's take this thing in and

get you back on shore, okay?" He then shakes his head in wonder. "Operation Dolphin Squad!"

A lot of things happen afterward that I just don't understand. Babushka, Tato, and I are escorted to a truck and taken to military police headquarters. Then, we're taken to the regular police headquarters, where Major Chaban shows up. I am sitting in the hallway—which is a lot like being outside Director Vovk's office, except much, much, much scarier. By the time Babushka and Tato reappear from behind a door, I am half-asleep on the bench, dressed in Babushka's cardigan and Tato's coat.

"Am I going to jail?" I ask, only half-awake.

"No," Tato says. "You're not going to jail."

And then I blink up at him, scared. "Are you?" I whisper.

He shakes his head and closes his eyes before asking, "Are you hungry?"

I am. I'm starving. Babushka puts an arm around my shoulders and steers me out into the parking lot. Some policeman drives us back to the dolphinarium. I blink. In the last strands of sunlight, I see that the building is barricaded behind hedgehogs and coils of razor wire. There are military patrol personnel stationed every few feet. Large signs state that it is now the property of the Russian Federation and the Russian navy.

Tato tells us to wait. He walks up to the soldiers, points at our orange Lada in the parking lot, and they let him through. When he returns with it, Babushka and I climb in.

"What are you hungry for?" Babushka asks me.

I look at Tato through the rearview mirror. "Can we just go to the food truck?"

I want to look out at the sea, too. I want to see what I can see beyond the summer-berry horizon.

Tato drives on the main road parallel to the promenade, then pulls up into the lot where Ivan's food truck is located.

Except nobody is there. Aside from some litter, the lot is empty.

The food truck is gone. The guard dogs are gone. Their cushions are gone. Ivan Markovych . . . is gone.

Tato slowly gets out of the car. Babushka is peering at him through the windshield. I jump out. I can't believe my eyes.

"Where is he?" I whisper hoarsely. "Where did he go?"

Tato looks toward that billboard. I see that someone has graffitied on it. *We are NOT one!* is now what it is says, and on the Russian flag, on the white part, they've painted *Slava Ukraïni!* Glory to Ukraine!

"He went east," Tato says, and kicks at a paper coffee cup. He stops and looks to the setting sun, then to the east again. "He's gone to fight. Just like he said he would."

I search the ground. There's a pile of paper napkins, taco wrappers, some plates, plastic bottles, a Dirol gum wrapper.

It's like I'm trying to categorize in biology.

Life > Domain > Kingdom > Phylum > Class > Order > Family > Genus > Species

Life in Sevastopol. Whose domain? Whose kingdom? And where are we in this order now? What is there left to categorize? Everyone's gone or leaving. Everyone I've ever cared about. Musty, Monk, and Marble. Ivan Markovych. Miss Yvette. Cedric will go back to Nigeria. Even Anna and Petro and their family have plans to move off the peninsula. Major Chaban is probably going to lock up Ilya in some tower and never let him out again. And the animals. Fizz is gone. The sea lions are gone. Even the dolphins are gone.

But Colin, Pesyk, Lily, and Roxi are at least safe.

I look at Tato and Babushka. I still have them. And of course I still have Neptune. As we pick through the litter like searching for clues, I suddenly spot one of those little yellow ribbons waving in the breeze on the willow tree. Those protest ribbons that are supposed to quietly say, "Crimea is Ukraine."

And there's something else. Something like a cardboard piece of paper. When I reach the trunk, I recognize what is tacked onto it. The postcard is faded, but I know that image well. It is the same postcard I received from my mother of the

Monument to the Sunken Ships. A Ukrainian flag is unfurled in the breeze. A ferry glides toward the west. I turn it over, almost expecting to find my mother's handwriting, her note about never returning.

But it's Ivan's chicken scratch and it's like he's written it to me, personally.

Until we meet again. And we <u>will</u> meet again.

CHAPTER 31

Until We Meet Again

Neptune is watching me through the window with narrowed eyes as I bring another box to the Lada. Tato takes it and adds it to the pile that Babushka is helping to strap onto the roof.

"I think that's it. We can put Neptune in the cat carrier," she says.

As it turns out, the only reason my tato and I were allowed to escape any charges is because Ilya agreed to let his father send him to a military school in Krasnodar. And my tato has agreed that he, Babushka, and I would get off the peninsula.

As long as Crimea remains under Russian occupation, we will never be allowed back.

I sigh and look at our little yellow house with the red shutters. I take in a deep breath of the sea air. Odesa is also on the sea, and I studied the photos of the dolphinarium there. Colin, Roxi, Pesyk, and Lily appear in news features and on their blog many times.

I hear the metal gate clang behind me. Cedric, Anna, and Petro are all on their bicycles. Cedric raises his hand to me, and I hurry over.

We do our secret handshake—all four of us—and then I lean against the fence.

"So, this is it?" Cedric asks.

I shake my head and reach over to hug him. Petro and Anna join us for a group hug, and I feel myself choke up. I'm going to miss my friends so much.

When I pull away, Petro retrieves his cell phone and waves it at me with a knowing look to all the others.

"Did you see this, Sofiya?" he asks at the same time as he pushes play on a YouTube video.

It's a news story about a Beluga whale found following a Norwegian ship. The whale appeared wearing a camera and a harness marked PROPERTY OF ST. PETERSBURG. A Russian spy whale.

Anna is smirking when I look up.

"Do you think it's Fizz?" I ask, excited.

"That's called going AWOL. Absent without official leave," she says.

"But the Kremlin refuses to acknowledge that he's their whale," Petro adds.

I laugh and look at the video again. I know for certain that it's Fizz. I could recognize him anywhere. Fizz, who's run away from Soviet trainers and ended up in Turkish waters.

Suddenly, Ilya appears, pushing into my street with his bicycle.

Excitement rushes over me again. "I thought you were in

Krasnodar," I say. I didn't think I'd have a chance to say goodbye to him.

"I leave tomorrow," Ilya says.

We all make room for him as he comes through the gate. He walks up to me and offers his hand. I'm feeling really grown up as I shake it. I think we're all taller, as a matter of fact.

"I wanted to say goodbye and good luck," Ilya says. He does the same with all the others. "And also, I thought you all might be interested in knowing that the Kremlin has decided that there will be a new training site for the military marine mammals at the old navy base since they've seized it from the Ukrainian navy." He glances at Petro and Anna with sympathy.

I let out a deep breath. What happened to Anna and Petro's father is awful. To all of our servicemen.

"But"—and Ilya nods toward Tato, still busy securing the car—"the dolphinarium will be reopened to the public at some point."

I shake my head. "It's too late." I point to the car. Babushka is coming out with Neptune yowling in the cat carrier. "We're going to be where our family is. In Odesa. Colin, Pesyk, Roxi, and Lily are waiting for us all."

Ilya smiles a little and looks me in the eye. "What are you going to do next?"

"Me? I'm going to be a scientist so I can put the world in order.

I'm also going to be an artist, like Miss Yvette said I should."

"Not a professional spy?" Cedric quips.

We all kind of laugh.

"And you?" I ask Ilya.

"I don't know." He scuffs the ground with his shoe, but when he looks back up, his eyes are glittering green. "As soon as I can, though, I'm going to leave the military. Maybe become an activist."

We all smile and Cedric pats his back. Anna and Petro fold their arms and lean back with identical expressions of admiration.

"I think we can always be activists," I say.

"Anyway," Ilya says, "I have to shove off."

I suddenly realize what I am leaving behind, and tears fill my eyes. "Promise me . . . all of you. We'll stay in touch?"

"Yeah," Ilya says. "Sure. Right?"

Everyone is nodding, and everyone's eyes are shining now.

Ilya's face blooms with a wide smile. He slowly lifts his arm and puts his hand in the center of our circle. "One last huddle?"

Anna drops her hand in at the same time as Petro. Next comes Cedric's. Mine lands on top. I grin at all my friends.

Quietly, like we're making a secret pact—like we're pinning our own yellow ribbons on Sevastopol and making a promise that we will do better—we whisper, *"Razom!"*

LATVIA
BALTIC
SEA
LITHUANIA
KALININGRAD
(RUSSIA)
BELARUS
POLAND
Lviv
Kyiv
UKRAINE
SLOVAKIA
Dnipro River
HUNGARY
MOLDOVA
Odesa
ROMANIA
U.S.
EUROPE
Area of
detail
ATLANTIC
OCEAN
CRIMEA
BLACK
Istanbul
TURKEY

BELARUS
RUSSIA
POLAND
Area held by Russia-backed separatists since 2014
Kyiv
OSCOW
UKRAINE
Dnipro River
Luhansk
Donetsk
MOLDOVA
SEA OF AZOV
ROMANIA
Annexed by Russia in 2014
CRIMEA
0 50 mi
0 80 km
BLACK SEA
RUSSIA
KAZAKHSTAN
N
W
E
S
SEA OF AZOV
CASPIAN SEA
0 100 mi
0 100 km
S E A
GEORGIA
AZERBAIJAN
ARMENIA

AFTERWORD

Starting in April 2014, war raged in Ukraine's eastern provinces, and Crimea was annexed and completely occupied by Russia. In May 2014, Ukraine voted in a pro-Western president to replace the president who had fled to Moscow after the Maidan. The West placed sanctions on Russia and called the annexation of the Crimean peninsula illegal.

In February 2022, when Sofiya, Ilya, Cedric, Anna, and Petro would have been around twenty years old, Russia launched a full-scale invasion on all of Ukraine. All of these fictional characters would have been old enough to enter the military and fight for their respective countries. Many of those Ukrainian teenagers who had protested at the Maidan with their parents were the first to enlist when Russia invaded. The death toll on both sides is horrifying and tragic.

This time, the United States, Canada, the United Kingdom, Europe, Japan, and hundreds of other countries did more than just place sanctions on Russia. They united behind Ukraine's right to defend itself. *Razom*—together—they have been working to help Ukraine fight for its sovereignty; in other words, no country has the right to invade another country just because it feels like it. And most especially when treaties are already in place, as they were between Russia and Ukraine.

This story is based on true events that took place in Sevastopol and at the dolphinarium there in 2014. I used this setting to shed light on the Russian-Ukrainian conflict and not to begin (or end) a debate about marine mammals in captivity.

The release of the Sevastopol dolphins into Ukrainian hands is purely fictional. However, the Russians did seize the dolphinarium in Sevastopol and ransomed the trainers and staff: Either they were to become Russian citizens and could continue working with the marine mammals or they would be banned from the facilities. Some staff and trainers complied, for whatever reasons they had. Rumors cropped up that the dolphins were not cooperating with their new Russian owners or went on hunger strikes in protest, and died. These stories seem implausible and remain unconfirmed. However, Russian government records show that five bottlenose dolphins were purchased and moved to the center in 2016. So what happened to the dolphins that were there in 2014?

Many factual stories and research helped to inspire the scenes for this novel. Although I take great pride in visiting all my settings, because of the war, I was unable to get to Sevastopol. I used, instead, pictures of the facilities from the internet, visited dolphinariums in Europe and North America, and created a fictional dolphinarium for the purposes of this book.

The movie *Dolphin Tale* (2011) inspired the setup of Sofiya's public viewing and social media ideas. It is based on Winter, a dolphin that was rescued and transferred to Clearwater Marine Aquarium in Florida. The research on dolphins and language at Kewalo Marine Laboratory in Hawaii inspired the sign language training in this story.

In 2022, under heavy shelling and bombardment, the staff of a dolphinarium in Kharkiv were able to move their animals to Odesa and later to a Romanian facility in Constanta. Both Ukrainian trainers and the animals now work there together and are doing well with their Romanian partners.

The ending of Sofiya's tale, though inspired by this true story, is fictional, of course, because simply releasing the dolphins into the wild would be an absolute no-no.

In the meantime, the Russian navy has been using military marine mammals in the Black Sea and in the Arctic for their purposes. Dolphins, seals, and whales patrol the waters for them, detect mines, lay mines, and are used to spy on commercial ships. Many Ukrainians hope to see the day when the Black Sea bottlenose dolphins are rescued from their fate, and are able to once more serve their purposes in peacetime:

for therapy, sharing knowledge, conducting research, and teaching people to love and respect sea life.

I am in deep gratitude to those who took the time to enlighten, teach, and share their expertise with me, especially the dolphins I was able to meet personally, and who helped create some of the most memorable and treasured experiences of my life.

GLOSSARY

Ukrainian	English
babushka	grandmother (mostly used by Russian-speaking people, but also Ukrainians)
dacha	a summer cottage in the country; many families have one but the sizes vary
dobre	fine; good
Donbas, Luhansk	two of Ukraine's eastern provinces, invaded and occupied by Russian separatists
khvist	tail
Klassno!	First class! Like, "Cool!" or "Super!"
kotyk(u)	kitten (term of endearment)
Kyiv	the capital of Ukraine, and also where the governing bodies are found
mama	mom or mother
Mova - (tse) nasha zbroya!	Language is our weapon!
Ni!	No!
Odesa	a Ukrainian city on the Black Sea

Pani doktorova	Ms. Doctor (can be used to address either a female doctor or the wife of a doctor)
pyrizhok or pyrizhky	jelly-filled pastry (singular) or jelly-filled pastries (plural)
rashist	a deragotory name for someone who is racist, Russian (and xenophobic)
Razom!	Together!
solodk(u)	Sweetheart
tato	dad or father
vulitsya Rybochka	Little Fish Street
vyshyvanka	embroidery; also refers to traditional clothing that contains embroidery

Russian	**English**
babushka	grandmother (mostly used by Russian-speaking people, but also Ukrainians)
dacha	a summer cottage in the country; many families have one but the sizes vary
khvost	tail
mat'	mom or mother
rashist	a deragotory name for someone who is racist, Russian (and xenophobic)

otets	dad or father
da	yes
Rossiya!	Russia!
Ya bol'she ne' vernus	I'm not (ever) coming back.
the Kremlin	the citadel, or walled area, where the governing bodies of Russia are found

Dolphin Terminology

beak	the dolphin's mouth
blowhole	the hole located at the top of the dolphin, allowing it to breathe and make its calls
dorsal fin	the fin at the top of the dolphin (like a shark fin)
experimental pool	a shallower pool used to get closer to the dolphins to study them or to do experiments on them
melon	the forehead of the dolphin, which modulates, focuses the animal's vocalizations, and locates sounds; used for communication and echolocation
military marine	a marine mammal trained for military

mammal	purposes
open-sea pen	a way to keep dolphins in the open sea but also held back from the open water
rostrum	the dolphin's mouth (top and bottom beak); can also be referred to as its snout
snout	see rostrum
spy-hop	a verticle half-rise out of the water performed by whales and dolphins so that they can view their surroundings above the surface of the water
staging area	usually the area where dolphins and marine mammals perform or learn their tricks for audiences
tail or fluke	the dolphin's tail end
waiting pool	some dolphinariums have multiple pools that hold the dolphins back before they enter the staging area (or staging pool)

ACKNOWLEDGMENTS

I am grateful to a number of people who assisted in this project, especially the eight- to twelve-year-old kids who took part in a role-play with me: Timo, Kvitka, Leo, Destiny, Jonathan, and William. Mostly strangers to one another, with some casual acquaintances, they were asked to work together—*razom!*—to fight back for the things they value most. Their interaction with one another was delightful and insightful!

Special thanks goes to Christiane for her openness and absolute generosity in standing ready for every question I might have. And for setting me straight before I could have gotten it so wrong.

I would never have been able to do this without my usual suspects and my growing squad. You know who you are. I am indebted to your services and support.

If this story has compelled you to contribute to Ukraine's effort against Russia's invasion, and especially to assist victims who have been displaced by the war, here is just one charity you might consider:

The Ukrainian Congress Committee of America https://ucca.org/donate/ For over 80 years, the UCCA has championed the interests of Ukrainian descendants in the USA through their non-profit, non-partisan community-based organizations. During Russia's war on Ukraine, the UCCA has utilized its vast worldwide network for supplying humanitarian and medical aid to people on the ground in Ukraine.

ABOUT THE AUTHOR

Chrystyna Lucyk-Berger is a Ukrainian-American who transplanted to Austria. She is the granddaughter of Ukrainian partisans and grandparents who survived a Nazi concentration camp.

Born in 1969, she grew up in the culture-rich neighborhood of "Nordeast" Minneapolis, part of the Ukrainian diaspora, and started her writing career with short stories, travel narratives, and poetry. She worked as a journalist and managing magazine editor, before jumping the desk and pursuing her own writing and traveling.

Her books tackle David-vs.-Goliath themes with strong women battling for the underdogs against a system, be it political, geographical, or industrial. Sometimes all three. "I enjoy discovering the good, the bad, and the ugly in my characters when they come into conflict," she says. "And all of my stories have been inspired by injustices I've discovered along my travels."

When she's not writing, Chrystyna works as a business communications trainer, consultant, and coach, developing educational programs, materials, and corporate training games. When she rests on her laurels, it's to spend quality time with family, friends, and her dog, two cats, and garden.